How to Play the King's Indian Defence

How to Play
the King's Indian Defence

DAVID LEVY and KEVIN O'CONNELL

B. T. Batsford Ltd *London*

First published 1980
© David Levy and Kevin O'Connell 1980

ISBN 0 7134 0759 X (cased)
ISBN 0 7134 0760 3 (limp)

Set by Hope Services, Abingdon
Printed in Great Britain
by Billing & Son Ltd
London, Guildford and Worcester
for the publishers
B. T. Batsford Limited
4 Fitzhardinge Street, London W1H 0AH

BATSFORD CHESS BOOKS
Adviser: R. G. Wade
Technical Editor: P. Lamford

CONTENTS

1 Introduction to the King's Indian Defence

The King's Indian Defence usually opens with the moves **1 P–Q4 N–KB3 2 P–QB4 P–KN3 3 N–QB3 B–N2**.

There was a time when this defence would arouse derision in all strong chess players because Black, during the first three moves, has done nothing to stake a firm claim in the centre, and classical chess theory requires both players to advance central pawns during the opening moves. In some openings, for example the Sicilian Defence (1 P–K4 P–QB4) and the Dutch Defence (1 P–Q4 P–KB4), Black does not advance a central pawn to the fourth rank but he does at least use one of his pawns to attack one of the central squares in White's half of the board (...Q5 or ...K5 respectively). In other defences, including the King's Indian, Black does not seek to contest the centre at once, but allows White to establish his pawn centre and then attempts to undermine it. It is clear from the above diagram, for example, that there is nothing to prevent White from playing an immediate P–K4, in which case he will have three pawns controlling central squares from the fourth rank while Black will have none. Our discussion of the King's Indian Defence is based on the various ways in which White seeks to occupy the centre with pawns, and the strategies which Black can adopt to oppose him.

White's fourth move in the King's Indian Defence is usually 4 P-K4, which not only increases his stake in the centre but also carries the threat of 5 P-K5, driving back the black knight from . . . KB3. It is interesting to note however, that Black can actually permit this advance and then attack the white pawn structure before White has had time to consolidate his position in the centre. The game Letelier-Fischer, Leipzig Olympiad 1960 continued: **(4 P-K4) O-O 5 P-K5 N-K1 6 P-B4 P-Q3** (striking at the White pawn centre) **7 B-K3 P-QB4!** (demolishing the centre) **8 QP×P N-QB3 9 BP×P P×P 10 N-K4 B-B4! 11 N-N3? B-K3 12 N-B3 Q-B2 13 Q-N1 P×P 14 P-KB5 P-K5! 15 P×B P×N 16 NP×P P-B4! 17 P-B4 N-B3 18 B-K2 KR-K1 19 K-B2 R×P 20 R-K1 QR-K1 21 B-B3 R×B! 22 R×R R×R 23 K×R Q×Pch!** White Resigns.

Even though P-K5 is not really a serious threat by White, it is normal for Black to play . . . P-Q3 at an early stage so as to support the advance of the KP and/or the QBP and to create development possibilities for Black's QB and QN. For this reason, the vast majority of King's Indian games include the moves **4 P-K4 P-Q3**, leading to the position shown in the following diagram.

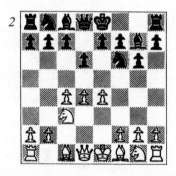

From this position White has a wide choice of variations, while Black's strategy is at first limited to a decision between playing for the thrust . . . P-K4 and . . . P-QB4. In this introduction we shall consider the various possibilities that arise after Black's first important decision.

Black plays for . . . P-K4

The moves . . . P-K4 and . . . P-QB4 have one important feature in common —they both lead, rather quickly, to positions in which the situation in the centre has been clarified. If White permits a pawn exchange on his Q4 square, the centre will remain fluid and it will be difficult for White to create play on the Q-side. The notable exception to this rule is in the fianchetto variations (see chapters 7 and 8) in which White's fundamental strategy does not revolve around a pawn advance on the Q-side.

✳ K×Q   24. Babott dummy!

Once Black advances a pawn to attack his opponent's Q4 square the choice for White normally lies between the advance of the QP to Q5, which creates a blocked centre, and the exchange of pawns which opens up the Q-file and often leads to an early endgame.

White meets . . . P–K4 with P–Q5

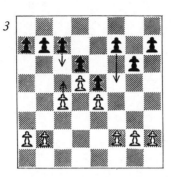

With the central pawns locked, the strategies of each side are easy to discern. White will try to force the advance P–QB5 under favourable circumstances and to create a strong Q-side attack. Black will counteract with . . . P–KB4 and a K-side attack, though occasionally the move . . . P–QB3 is a useful means of weakening White's pawn centre. Let us first examine an example of a successful Q-side attack by White.

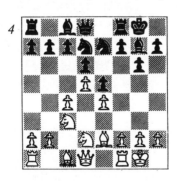

Kaplan–Mayer   U.S.A. 1978

10 P–QN4 P–KB4 Both sides begin their thematic advances without hesitation. **11 P–B5** A pawn sacrifice which Black does best to decline. After 11 . . . QP×P 12 NP×P N×BP 13 B–R3, White has a very active game for the pawn. **11 . . . N–KB3 12 P–B3 P–B5 13 N–B4 P–KN4 14 B–R3** QR3 is often a useful square for White's QB since from there the bishop increases the pressure on Black's Q3 pawn and introduces latent threats against the rook on ... KB1. **14 ... N–K1 15 Q–N3 N–N3 16 QR–B1 P–KR4 17 P–R3 R–B2 18 N–Q1 B–B1?** ... KB3 would be a better square for the bishop. **19 N–B2 R–N2 20 R–B2 N–R5 21 KR–B1 N–B3**

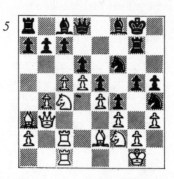

White's Q-side attack is poised to break through while Black's K-side counterplay is going nowhere. **22 P×P P×P 23 P–N5 P–N5** Otherwise Black will get squashed on the Q-side. **24 BP×P P×P 25 P×P N(B3)×NP 26 N×N B×N 27 B×B R×B 28 Q–R3!** Surprise, surprise. Black's K-side counterattack was launched with insufficient force behind it, permitting White a simple tactical blow. If 28 ... R–N3 29 N×KP! P×N 30 B×B, winning a vital pawn, and if 30 ... K×B or 30 ... Q×B then 31 R–B8 wins the queen for a rook and minor piece, White's domination of the QB-file finally coming into its own. **28 ... Q–N4 29 B×P P–B6 30 N×P R–B5** The tempting 30 ... R×P+ 31 R×R N×R is met by 32 Q–K6+, winning at once. **31 Q–K6+ K–R1 32 N–B7+ Black Resigns**.

Let us now look at what happens when Black mounts his K-side counterattack in a more careful manner.

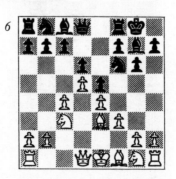

Bobotsov–Gligorić   Amsterdam 1971
7 ... P–B3 A thematic move which reduces the strength of White's central pawn mass. White can rarely afford to meet ... P–QB3 with QP×P because

after Black recaptures with the QNP it will be easy for Black to achieve counterplay by means of an eventual . . . P-Q4. White must therefore submit to the exchange of pawns on his Q5 square. **8 B-Q3 P×P 9 BP×P** Recapturing with the KP would be a grave strategic error in this type of position since it would add force to the eventual advance . . . P-KB4 by Black. In recapturing with the QBP White loses one of the traditional motifs of the Q-side attack, namely the advance P-QB5, but in return he has opened the QB-file for eventual occupation by his rooks. **9 . . . QN-Q2 10 KN-K2 N-B4** The manoeuvre . . . QN-Q2 followed by . . . N-QB4 is often seen in positions with this particular pawn structure (white pawns on QB4, Q5, K4 v black pawns on . . . QB2, . . . Q3 and . . . K4). In order that the move . . . N-QB4 cannot be met by an immediate P-QN4, driving away the knight, it is important that on . . . QB4 the knight carries some threat. Often the threat is simply to win the white KP, which is attacked by both black knights, but in this case the white KP is rather well protected. Here, however, Black threatens to exchange his knight for White's Q3 bishop, and so before he can contemplate driving away the knight White must retreat his bishop. **11 B-QB2 P-QR4** This is the usual follow-up to the knight manoeuvre—Black prevents P-QN4 so that his knight can remain on . . . QB4 for a while. **12 0-0 B-Q2 13 P-QR3 N-R4 14 P-QN4 P×P 15 P×P N-R3 16 R-N1 N-B5** There is no need for White to fear 17 N×N or 17 B×N, since the recapture with the KP opens up the diagonal for Black's KB, attacking White's QB3. **17 Q-Q2 R-B1 18 KR-B1 R-B5 19 N-R2**

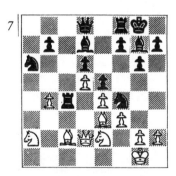

7

19 . . . **P-B4 20 P×P B×P 21 B×B N×N+ 22 Q×N R×R+ 23 R×R P×B** It is a golden rule that Black should recapture with the KNP unless there exists an extremely good reason for not doing so. The pawns on . . . K4 and . . . KB4 form an imposing pair and can support each other's advance. In addition, Black is often able to launch an attack along the semi-open KN-file. **24 Q-N5 Q-K2 25 Q-N6 P-B5! 26 B-B2 P-K5! 27 P×P P-B6! 28 Q-K3 P×P 29 K×P Q-B3**. The position is approximately equal and was drawn in 42 moves.

Black plays for . . . QB4

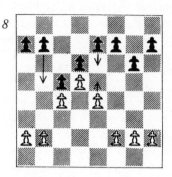

8

The pawn formation in the above diagram offers each side completely different possibilities to those seen when Black has pawns on . . . K4 and . . . QB2 rather than . . . K2 and . . . QB4. Here White cannot hope to advance his QBP, but he does have the possible break P–K5 at his disposal, provided that he can add support to the K5 square with moves such as P–KB4, R–K1, B–KB4 and/or N–KB3. In fact, in positions with this central pawn structure, the move P–K5 is usually White's principal aim.

There are two popular methods for attacking the white pawn centre. The more straightforward of these is to attack the head of the pawn phalanx by . . . P–K3, when White must choose between exchanging pawns on K6 and permitting the exchange on his Q5. The less direct approach involves the move . . . P–QN4, which strikes at the most vulnerable point in White's pawn centre. Once White's QBP has been traded for Black's QNP Black will have attacking possibilities along the .QN-file and White's Q5 pawn will have lost much of its support. If an endgame is reached, in which White has only his KP guarding Q5, Black can undermine the QP still further by means of the thrust . . . P–KB4.

These three themes, the advance of White's KP and Black's . . . P–QN4 and . . . P–K3, can occur independently or together. Here are some examples.

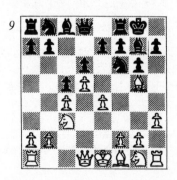

9

Suba–Uhlmann   Bucharest 1978

7 ... P-K3 8 B-Q3 P×P 9 KP×P The recapture on Q5 is almost inevitably made with either the KP or the QBP. If 9 N×P QN-Q2, and there is no way for White to capitalize on the pin. **9 ... R-K1+ 10 KN-K2 P-KR3 11 B-R4 N-R3** When White meets ... P-QB4 with P-Q5 in King's Indian positions, it is often possible for Black to create Q-side counterplay by developing his QN via ... QR3 to ... QB2, from where it can support the advance of the QNP. Here the knight serves a dual function – it can jump in to ... QN5 to displace the white bishop. **12 0-0 B-Q2 13 P-B4 Q-N3 14 P-B5 P-N4 15 B-KB2?** The bishop would be more active on KN3, attacking the black QP. **15 ... Q×P** This move required exact calculation, since it permits White's rook to enter on the seventh rank. **16 R-N1 Q-R6 17 R×P N-QN5! 18 B-N1 B-QB1** ‡8 ... Q-R3 also wins rook for bishop, but allows White more counterplay than in the game. **19 R-N5 B-R3 20 R-K1 QR-Q1 21 Q-Q2 B×R 22 N×B Q-R4 23 B-N3** 23 P-R3 can be met by 23 ... N-B3, when White's queen is attacked. **23 ... Q-N3 24 N(K2)-B3** Not 24 P-R3 N(B3)×P! **24 ... R×R+ 25 Q×R P-R3 26 N×P R×N 27 B×R Q×B 28 P-R3 Q-B5! 29 P×N P×P** The counter sacrifice has left Black with a decisive advantage because of his passed Q-side pawns and his more active minor pieces. **30 N-K4 N×N 31 B×N** If 31 Q×N B-Q5+ 32 K-R1 Q-KB8+ 33 K-R2 B-N8+ and White's king will be hounded to death. **31 ... B-B6 32 P-N3** Or 32 Q-K2 B-Q5+ 33 K-R1 Q-QB8+, again with a winning attack. It is one of the great paradoxes in chess that the motif of opposite coloured bishops, which is so helpful to the defending side in the endgame, is often the cause of defeat when queens are on the board. **32 ... Q-K4 33 Q-N1 Q×NP+ 34 B-N2 P-N6 35 P-Q6 B-Q5+ 36 K-R1 B-K4 37 K-N1 B×P 38 P-B6 Q-K6+ 39 K-R1 P-N7** White Resigns.

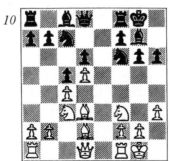

10

Ree–Minić   Karlovac 1977

Here White has again recaptured on Q5 with the KP. When this happens Black need not fear the attack instituted by the advance P-K5 and so his defensive task is normally somewhat easier. **12 ... P–QN4! 13 P–QN3** After 13 P×P B–N2 or 13 N×P N×N 14 P×N B–N2, Black can pick up the QP at will. **13 ... R–K1 14 Q–B2 R–N1 15 QR–K1 P×P 16 P×P B–Q2?** Black should first exchange rooks, to make his position less constricted, and then develop the QB. **17 R–N1 N–R3 18 P–R3 Q–K2 19 B–B4 N–R4 20 B–R2 P–B4 21 N–QN5 B×N 22 R×B R×R?** This hands complete control of the Q-side over to White. Better was 22 ... N–B2. **23 P×R N–B2 24 Q–R4 N–R1 25 R–K1 Q×R+** Desperation, but if 25 ... Q–B2 26 R×R+ Q×R 27 Q×P, Black is hopelessly lost. **26 N×Q R×N+ 27 B–B1 N–N3 28 Q×P N–QB5 29 P–N4 N–Q7 30 P×N** and White won.

11

Gligorić–Tringov   Osijek 1978
White has recaptured on Q5 with the QBP, announcing his intention to attack on the K-side and to play for the advance P–K5. Note that White has already played P–QR4, inhibiting ... P–QN4, with the result that Black is almost starved of counterplay. **12 ... R–K1 13 B–K3 R–N1 14 Q–Q2 N–N3** Black hopes to encourage P–QR5, with the idea that once the knight retreats from ... QN3 Black will be ready to play ... P–QN4, and on P×P e.p. Black can recapture with the queen and invade the Q-side with his heavy pieces. The idea is a reasonable one but in this position it is too slow. **15 B–R6 B–R1 16 P–B4 KN–Q2 17 P–R5 N–R1 18 P–K5!** The thematic breakthrough. **18 ... P×P 19 P–Q6 Q–Q1 20 B–B4 N–B1** 20 ... P–QN4 looks tempting, but then comes 21 B×BP+! K×B 22 Q–Q5+ R–K3 23 N(B2)–K4, threatening 24 N–KN5+ as well as 24 P×P+ **21 B–KN5 Q–Q2 22 N(B2)–K4 P×P 23 R×P N–K3 24 N–B6+ B×N 25 R×B P–N4** At last, but too late. **26 B×N R×B 27 R×R** Black Resigns 27 ... Q×R allows the white rook to infiltrate to the seventh rank by 28 R–K1 Q–Q2 29 R–K7, while 27 ... P×R 28 N–K4 will be followed by N–B6 and P–Q7, etc.

12

Portisch-Spassky   6th Match Game 1977

In the previous example Black's counterplay with ... P-QN4 never got moving in time and he was squashed on the K-side and in the centre. Let us now look at the sort of thing that can happen when a well played central breakthrough meets a well played Q-side counterattack. Once again, White has recaptured on Q5 with his QBP. **11 ... B-N5**

By putting pressure on White's KB3 knight Black reduces White's control over the K5 square, thereby making the advance P-K5 more difficult to achieve. In positions with this pawn structure Black does not normally object to exchanging his QB for White's KN. **12 0-0 QN-Q2 13 P-R3 B×N 14 B×B P-B5** This pawn looks vulnerable on ... QB5 but in compensation Black has the use of ... QB4 for his knight. Also, Black can forsee an eventual ... P-QN4, which will protect the pawn on ... QB5. **15 N-N5 Q-N3 16 B-K3 N-B4 17 N-R3 Q-N5 18 R-B1** If 18 Q-B1 N-N6, and White will not get enough compensation for the exchange. **18 ... P-QN4 19 P×P P×P 20 N-B2 Q×P 21 R-N1 Q-K4 22 B-Q4** White can regain the pawn by 22 R×P but then 22 ... N-N6 leaves Black with the more active position. **22 ... Q-K1 23 P-K5 N(B3)-Q2 24 P×P N-N6! 25 B×B K×B 26 R-K1 Q-N1 27 N-Q4 N(Q2)-B4 28 N-K6+! P×N 29 P×P** In return for the piece White has two strong connected passed pawns. The immediate threat is simply B×R. **29 ... R-R3 30 P-K7 R-K1 31 R×N!** White would dearly like to give check with his queen on QR1 or Q4. If now 31 ... R×QP? 32 Q-R1+ K-B2 33 R-R3 and 34 R-R8 will win; or if 31 ... P×R 32 Q-Q4+ K-R3 33 Q-B4+ K-N2 34 Q-K5+ K-R3 35 P-N4 N-K3 36 P-R4, and Black is in a mating net. So Black has no choice; **31 ... Q×P** Keeping guard on both ... QR8 and ... Q5. **34 Q×Q R×Q 33 R×P N-Q6 34 R-K2 K-B3 35 R-N7 R-K3 36 R-B2 R(1)×P 37 R×R R×R** and the players soon agreed to a draw. The ending with all the pawns on the same side is a book draw.

By now the reader should be convinced that ... P-QN4 is a vital ingredient of Black's counterplay in positions with a white pawn on Q5 and black pawns on ... Q3 and ... QB4. The manner in which Black attempts to achieve this break is often of crucial importance, since the wrong approach to the problem will often enable White to prevent ... P-QN4, or at least to ensure that it is ineffectual.

13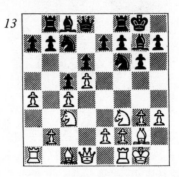

Let us first examine the direct **10 ... P-QR3** Black is now ready for the break ... P-QN4 since he has as many pieces defending that square (the pawn on ... QR3, the knight on ... QB2 and the rook on ... QN1) as White has attacking it (pawns on QR4 and QB4, knight on QB3). **11 P-R5** The normal reaction to ... P-QR3. Now, when Black advances the QNP, White can exchange pawns on QN6 so that Black cannot recapture with the QRP. **11 ... P-QN4 12 PXP e.p. RXP 13 N-Q2 P-K3 14 N-N3 PXP 15 PXP B-Q2 16 N-R5** White has the advantage because of the active position of his knight on QR5.

In contrast, we shall now examine a more subtle but somewhat slower solution. **10 ... P-QN3** Now, if Black is given time for ... P-QR3, White will not be able to answer P-R5 because of the reply ... P-QN4, when Black has achieved his aim of establishing an active QNP. **11 P-K4 P-QR3 12 P-K5** Worried about the possibility of the imminent break on the Q-side, White attempts to create something in the centre. **12 ... N-Q2 13 PXP PXP 14 B-N5 P-B3 15 B-B4 N-K1 16 P-R4** Directed against Black's expansion on the K-side by ... P-KN4. **16 ... N-K4 17 N-Q2 N-KB2 18 R-K1 P-KN4 19 PXP PXP 20 B-K3 N-K4 21 N(B3)-K4 P-R3 22 R-R3 N-N5** As a general rule in the King's Indian, Black does well to exchange off White's dark squared bishop for a knight, since this enhances the effectiveness of his own KB. Black has a completely satisfactory position.

Having discussed the various possibilities that arise when, after White's advance P-Q5, Black plays ... P-K3 and KPXP, we should now consider what may happen when White does not wait for ... KPXP but instead makes the capture QPXKP. Black then has the option of recapturing with the QB or the KBP, both of which can lead to sharp play. As a general rule players of the white pieces usually prefer to delay the fireworks until they have built up a solid position, and the capture on White's K6 square is therefore a comparative rarity in master chess.

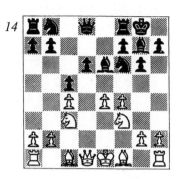

14

Bukhman–Karasev Leningrad Ch 1967

9 B–Q3 The logical square for the bishop: it can support the advance of the KBP which wil be an important part of White's attack. **9 . . . N–B3 10 P–B5 B–Q2 11 0–0 N–KN5** Hoping to create chances on the dark squares (. . . K4 and . . . Q5). **12 B–N5 B–Q5+ 13 K–R1 P–B3 14 N×B P×N** Naturally not 14 . . . P×B 15 N×N and 16 Q×N, winning a piece. **15 Q×N P×N 16 B–R6** White has a strong attack, thanks partly to the absence of Black's dark squared bishop.

So far our discussion of King's Indian positions has centred around the pawn formations in which White has pawns on QB4, Q5 and possibly K4, while Black has played . . . P–Q3 and either . . . P–QB4 or . . . P–K4. It should be mentioned that Black has one further option: he can advance both his KP and his QBP to the fourth rank.

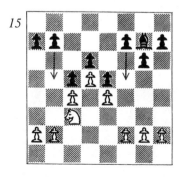

15

In this type of position Black has accepted a disadvantage in space but he need not fear the advance of White's KP or the QBP which, as we have seen, form the principal breaks at White's disposal. With pawns on . . . QB4 and . . . K4, Black hopes to compensate for his disadvantage in space by increasing the number of pawn breaks at his disposal from one to two, since he can now hope for ... P-QN4 and/or ... P-KB4. In practice it is often found that White's extra manoeuverability, and the difficulty experienced by Black in switching his forces from one flank to the other, will give White the advantage.

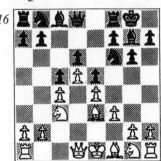

16

Hort–Gligorić   Niksic 1978

8 B-Q3 N-R4 9 KN-K2 P-B4 The first pawn break. **10 P×P P×P 11 Q-Q2 P-QR3 12 P-QR4** Preventing ... P-QN4. **12 ... N-Q2 13 B-N5 Q-K1 14 0-0 N(Q2)-B3 15 B-B2 B-Q2 16 QR-N1 Q-B1** Black is not yet ready for ... P-QN4 because of 17 RP×P P×P 18 N×P, and if 18 ... B×N 19 P×B Q×P then 20 B×P, winning **P-QR3. 17 P-R5** Preventing ... P-N4. For this reason Black should have played ... P-N3 before ... Q-B1. **17 ... Q-B2 18 N-R4 P-K5 19 N-N6 QR-K1 20 R(N1)-K1 K-R1 21 K-R1 R-KN1 22 N-B4 N×N 23 Q×N R(K1)-KB1 24 Q-R4 B-K1 25 P×P N×P 26 B-Q8 Q-N1 27 B-K7 R-B2 28 B×N P×B 29 Q×KP B×NP 30 R×R B×R 31 Q-B4 B-N3 32 N-Q7 Q-B2 33 B-B6+ Black Resigns** because of 33 ... B×B 34 Q×B+ R-N2 35 R-K7. It was White who won on the K-side.

We have now finished our introduction to those positions in which White meets ... P-QB4 or ... P-K4 by advancing his QP to the fifth rank, and it only remains for us to take a brief look at the possibility of exchanging pawns on QB5 or K5 instead of advancing the QP.

17

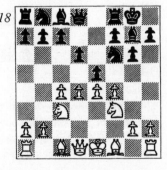

18

In diagram 17 it is easy to see that after **7 P×P P×P 8 Q×Q R×Q**, there is no future in **9 N×P?** because Black can win back the pawn with the better game by **9 . . . N×P!**

The position in diagram 18 is completely different, but only because of a number of tactical devices. Watch the play and the analysis closely. **7 QP×P P×P 8 Q×Q R×Q 9 N×P** After 9 P×P N–N5 10 B–B4 R–K1, White will not be able to keep the pawn. **9 . . . R–K1 10 B–Q3 N×P** With this temporary piece sacrifice Black hopes to regain the pawn with a satisfactory position. **11 B×N!** 11 N×N P–KB3 plays right into Black's hands. **11 . . . P–KB3 12 B–Q5+ K–R1** If 12 . . . K–B1 13 0–0! P×N 14 P×P+ B–B4 (forced) 15 P–KN4. **13 B–B7 R–B1 14 N×P+ P×N 15 B×KNP** White is two pawns up with a won game.

We have given these two positions side by side to show that in general White cannot expect to profit from the pawn grab on K5, but that sometimes Black must calculate the tactics very carefully to ensure that he can regain the pawn.

Finally, we consider the capture of Black's QBP after the move . . . P–QB4.

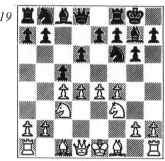

Johannessen–Tal   Reykjavik 1964

7 P×P Q–R4! This motif is well known from similar positions in other openings, for example the Pirc Defence and some variations of the Sicilian. The pin on White's QB3 knight imposes a direct threat to the KP. **8 B–Q3 KN–Q2 9 B–Q2 N×P 10 B–B2 Q–N5** Already Black has regained the pawn and snatched the initiative. **11 B–N3 Q–N3 12 Q–K2** Turning a bad position into a hopeless one. White's most serious problems were the threat of . . . N–Q6+ and his inability to castle. **12 . . . N×B 13 N–Q5 Q–R3 14 R–Q1** Or 14 N–B7 Q–R5. **14 . . . Q×RP 15 N–B7 N–R3** White Resigns. The knight on QR8 will be lost and Black will be left with the winning material advantage of two minor pieces and a pawn for a rook. This sort of catastrophe is not inevitable after QP×P in the King's Indian but it is a fitting example with which to end our introduction to one of the most interesting defences to 1 P–Q4.

2 The Four Pawns Attack

Since Black does not advance any of his pawns to the fourth rank during the first few moves of the King's Indian, it is possible for White to build a very broad pawn centre by placing his QP, QBP, KP and KBP on the four key squares Q4, QB4, K4 and KB4. This set-up is known as the Four Pawns Attack.

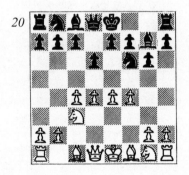

20

Fifty years ago, when an impressive looking pawn centre was usually regarded as a great advantage, White used to win many games by adopting this strategy. Over the past few decades however, we have learned that in many openings, not only the King's Indian, a broad pawn centre is not necessarily something to be feared. In fact, many players prefer to play against an imposing looking pawn centre because it gives them an immediate target for attack.

Before we examine the most sensible methods of defence against the Four Pawns Attack, it would be as well to illustrate White's attacking possibilities with some examples from master games, just in case the reader gets the impression that White's pawn advances are little more than a gesture.

21

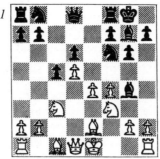

Liptay-Bukić   Krakow 1964

10 P-K5 The advances P-K5 and P-KB5 are the two most important pawn thrusts in White's plans in the Four Pawns Attack. The strategy is to combine a central breakthrough with a steady build up on the king's wing, culminating in a mating attack against the black king. **10 . . . N-K1?** Passive. Black should exchange pawns and then retreat the knight to the more active square . . . Q2, from where it exerts some influence on the key square . . . K4. Note the similarity between this position and many of those arising in the Modern Benoni (see pages 92-101), where control of White's K5 square is vital. **11 N-KN5 B×B 12 Q×B N-B2?** Another feeble move. Black should play 12 . . . Q-K2 so as to keep . . . K4 under observation. **13 0-0 Q-K2 14 N(B3)-K4!** Not only attacking the Q6 pawn, but also the important square KB6. **14 . . . N-K1 15 B-K3 N-R3 16 Q-B3 P-R3 17 Q-R3 P×P** Naturally not 17 . . . P×N 18 N×NP, when Black must resign because of the mate threat at . . . KR2. **18 P-B5!** The other thematic pawn push. **18 . . . P×N 19 P-B6!** Now 19 N×NP can be answered by 19 . . . N-B3, so White simply regains the piece. If 19 . . . N×P 20 B×NP. **19 . . . B×P 20 R×B! K-N2** Or 20 . . . N×R 21 B×NP. **21 B×NP R-R1 22 Q-K3 Q-Q2 23 QR-KB1 Q×P 24 Q-Q2!** N(R3)-B2 If 24 . . . Q×N 25 R×BPch K-N1 26 R-B8ch K-R2 27 Q-Q7ch leads to a mating attack. **25 Q×Q N×Q 26 R×BPch K-N1 27 R-B8ch K-R2 28 R(1)-B7ch N-N2 29 R×QR R×R 30 N-B6ch N×N 31 B×N R-KN1 32 R×P K-R3 33 B×P N-B4 34 R×P** and White won with his two extra pawns.

22

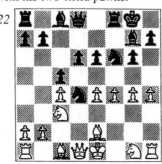

Mariotti–Gligorić   Praia da Rocha 1969
Here White has taken things a little far! His 'six pawn attack' looks more
suitable for a 5-minute game than for a serious international competition,
and Mariotti's illustrious opponent, one of the world's leading experts on
the King's Indian Defence, assumed that there was nothing much for Black
to worry about. But look at what happens. **11 P–R5 P–Q4?** The normal
response to a premature flank attack is a counter-thrust in the centre, but
here Black plays too automatically. Correct was 11 . . . P–QN4!, and if 12
P×KNP? then 12 . . . P–N5! is good for Black because the white knight is
driven from its defence of the KP and Black will crash through in the
centre. **12 P–K5 N–K5 13 RP×P RP×P 14 Q–Q3 P–QN4 15 N×N NP×P
16 Q–KR3 P×N 17 Q–R7ch K–B2 18 P–B5! KP×P 19 R–R6 N–B7ch 20
K–B1 P×P 21 K–N2 N–K8ch 22 K–R1 N–Q6 23 Q×Pch K–N1 24 Q–R7ch
K–B2 25 B–K3 Q–K2 26 R–KB1ch K–K1 27 Q–N6ch R–B2 28 Q–QB6ch
Q–Q2 29 R–K6ch K–B1 30 B×BPch N×B 31 Q×Nch K–N1 32 R–Q6
Q–N2 33 R×R K×R 34 B×BPch K–K1 35 B–Q5 Q–K2 36 Q–B6ch K–B1
37 Q×R Q–R5ch 38 K–N2 Black Resigns**

There are two important lessons to be learned from these examples.
Firstly, Black must always be prepared to meet the pawn advances P–K5
and/or P–KB5. If these advances can be played with impunity, White will
usually be able to utilize his central space advantage by bringing his piece
over to the K-side in preparation for a mating attack. In particular, once
White has achieved P–K5, his QB3 knight is ready to jump in to K4 from
where it can eye both KB6 and KN5.

Secondly, Black must never underestimate the potential of White's
K-side attack. Black's counterplay must be swift and sure footed, otherwise
it will not distract White from his attacking ambitions. The two natural
counter-attacking moves against a Four Pawns type attack are . . . P–Q4
and . . . P–QN4. Gligoric chose the wrong one against Mariotti and we have
already seen the result. In the examples that follow, the reader will be able
to see the effectiveness of . . . P–QN4 as an antidote to the attack; the
move . . . P–Q4 is not always possible because in many lines White maintains
a pawn of his own on that square.

Typical pawn structures in the Four Pawns Attack
After the opening moves: 1 P–Q4 N–KB3 2 P–QB4 P–KN3 3 N–QB3 B–N2
4 P–K4 P–Q3 5 P–B4 0–0 6 N–B3, Black almost always replies 6 . . .
P–QB4. It is then possible for a number of different pawn formations to
arise, depending on how White chooses to play the position. If White does
not advance his QP at once, Black will exchange pawns on . . . Q5, thereby
bringing about a position reminiscent of the Maroczy Bind in the Sicilian
Defence. (The reader is referred to chapter 2 of our companion volume

How to play the Sicilian Defence, for a full discussion of Maroczy positions in which Black has fianchettoed his KB.)

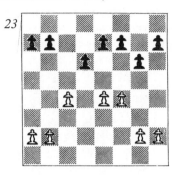

If White does advance his QP at once, which is the most common way of playing the position, Black's first task is to resolve the central pawn structure by means of . . . P-K3, when White must either exchange pawns on K6 or permit Black to exchange on Q5. If White decides to exchange pawns on K6 he will remain with pawns on QB4, K4 and KB4. Otherwise Black will play . . . KPxP and White will recapture with the QBP or the KP, producing one or other of the following pawnstructures.

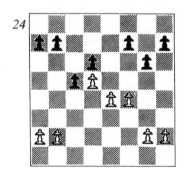

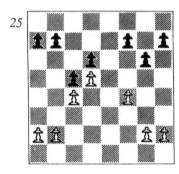

These three different pawnstructures each require their own individual treatment, and so it is not possible for us to give thematic ideas or golden rules which can equally be applied to all of them. We shall therefore depart from our usual approach, and for the remainder of this chapter we will discuss a number of examples from tournament play so that the reader will be able to follow the typical plans that are employed with these pawnstructures.

White does not advance P-Q5

As we have already mentioned, if Black gets the chance to do so he should exchange his QBP for White's QP. The resulting position is reminiscent of the Maroczy Bind in the Sicilian Defence, but with the important difference that here White's KBP has moved beyond the third rank and therefore the white KP is more vulnerable than usual in such situations. Black plays the positions in much the same way that he plays against the Maroczy Bind in chapter 2 of *How to play The Sicilian Defence*.

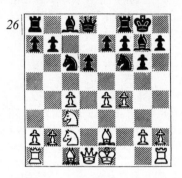

Kopayev–Gusev   Lvov 1951

9 ... B–K3 As in the Maroczy Sicilian, this is the most active square for the bishop, which helps to support Black's minority attack on the Q-side. On ... Q2 the bishop would be vulnerable to the advance P–K5 or P–QB5 in certain positions. **10 0–0 R–B1 11 B–K3** 11 P–KB5 is not really dangerous because it gives Black the fine square ... K4 for his knight. **11 ... P–QR3 12 R–B1 Q–R4 13 K–R1 P–QN4!** Already Black has a good game. The vulnerability of White's KP is shown by the variation 14 P×P P×P 15 B×P N×P, when White's Q-side is under very strong pressure.

White advances P–Q5 and meets ... P–K3 with P×KP

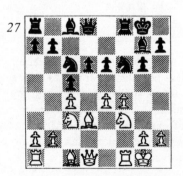

S. Garcia–Tatai   Bucharest 1971

Here Black has recaptured on ... K3 with the KBP. This had two advantages over the recapture ... QB×P: firstly, the black bishop on ... K3 is often vulnerable to the advance P-KB5, which comes with gain of tempo and therefore speeds up White's K-side attack; secondly, with a pawn on ... K3 rather than a bishop, it will be easier for Black to force the thematic break ... P-Q4. Tatai now played **10 ... N-Q5?!** This reduces Black's control over the ... K4 square and makes it easier for White to force the advance P-K5. 10 ... P-QR3 was a safe alternative. **11 N-KN5** Already P-K5 is a threat, and once·Black's knight has been driven away from ... KB3 it may be possible for White to sacrifice with N×KRP K×N; Q-R5ch and Q×KNP. **11 ... Q-K2 12 Q-K1 B-Q2 13 Q-R4?!** 13 B-Q2 would be less ambitious but probably sounder. **13 ... QR-K1?** Too slow. Black should have played 13 ... N-R4! intending ... P-KR3 and the exchange of queens, e.g. 14 P-KN4 P-KR3 15 P×N P×N, and Black has the more active position. **14 B-Q2 B-B3 15 P-K5 P×P 16 P×P N-R4 17 P-KN4 B×P** 17 ... P-KR3 can be met by 18 B×P P×N 19 Q×N, winning material and remaining with a strong attack. **18 P×N N-B4 19 B×N B-Q5ch 20 Q×B!!** White had been planning this queen sacrifice since 13 Q-R4. **20 ... P×Q 21 B×KPch K-N2 22 N-Q5 B×N 23 P-R6ch! K×P 24 N-B7dbl ch K-R4** After 24 ... K-N2 25 B-R6ch K-N1 26 P×B, White will win with ease. **25 P×B Q-B4 26 QR-B1 Q-N4 27 QR-K1 P-N4 28 R-B6 R×B 29 P×R Q×P 30 P-K7** 30 R-R6ch forces mate in two more moves. **30 ... R-K1 31 P-KR3 K-R5 32 R-K4ch K-N6 33 B-K1ch** Black resigns. A beautiful example of White's attacking possibilities when Black fails to maintain sufficient influence in the centre. The black knight on ... Q5 never did accomplish anything.

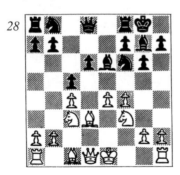

28

Lombardy-Westerinen   Lone Pine 1978

When Black has recaptured on ... K3 with the bishop he must always beware of the possibility of P-KB5 by White. Here, for example, Black would do well to continue with 9 ... B-N5, so as to exchange off the light squared bishop before it is shut in by the advance of the white KBP. The exchange of Black's bishop for White's KB3 knight removes one of White's key attacking pieces from the board and weakens White's control of the important central square K5 and Q4. **9 . . . N–B3?! 10 P–B5! B–Q2 11 0–0 N–QN5?!** As in the previous example Black relinquishes some of his central control. 11 . . . R–K1 would be more circumspect. **12 B–N1 B–B3 13 P–QR3 N–R3 14 B–N5 N–B2?** Black had to play 14 . . . P–KR3 to prevent the exchange of dark squared bishops. **15 Q–Q2 Q–Q2 16 B–B2 P–QN4** This move often represents Black's best route to counterplay but here it is inadequate because White already has too strong an attack. **17 QR–Q1 N(3)–K1 18 B–R6!** P×P **19** B×B K×B **20 P–K5!** P–Q4 **21 P–B6ch K–N1** Now White has control of the dark squares around Black's king and a mating attack is almost inevitable. **22 P–R3!** To keep the black queen out of KN4. **22 . . . P–Q5 23 N–K4 N–K3 24 Q–R6** B×N Otherwise 25 N–N5 would force mate. **25** B×B **R–N1 26 N–R4!** P–Q6 Otherwise 27 R–B5 is strong, with the killing threat of 28 R–R5! **27 N–B5! K–R1 28 R–B4** Black resigns because of the threat of 29 R–R4.

In both of these examples we saw how important it is for Black to retain his influence in the centre and to watch White's K-side build up very carefully, lest it should become overwhelming.

White advances P–Q5 and permits Black to exchange pawns, recapturing with the QBP

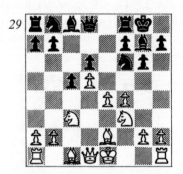

29

Michalev–Petrayev   Novosibirsk 1967

We have already seen one example of this particular pawn structure in the Liptay–Bukic game on page 15. Since this formation arises more often than any other in the Four Pawns Attack, it would be as well for the reader to study the present game, so as to have a deeper understanding of the dynamic counter-chances at Black's disposal. The reader should also note the similarity between this type of position and many Modern Benoni positions. In both cases White's strategy revolves around the advances P–K5 and/or P–KB5, while Black often seeks counterplay by means of the Q-side thrust . . . P–QN4.

9 . . . P–QN4 The most dynamic continuation, though Black can also play 9... R–K1, restraining the advance of the white KP. **10 P–K5** If White grabs the pawn his king is displaced and Black's attacking possibilities will probably provide sufficient compensation, e.g. 10 B×P N×KP 11 N×N Q–R4ch 12 K–B2 Q×B 13 N×QP Q–N3. **10 ... P×P 11 P×P N–N5 12 B–KB4** 12 B–N5 appears to be more aggressive, but after 12 ... P–B3 White's advanced pawn duo will disintegrate. The text move aims to keep control of K5, the most vital square in positions of this sort. **12 ... P–N5! 13 N–K4 N–Q2 14 P–K6** The only way for White to justify his choice of opening variation is to press on with the pawns. **14 ... P×P 15 P×P R×B 16 Q–Q5 K–R1** Forced. **17 R–Q1** 17 Q×R N–N3 18 Q–B6 N–K6 is amazingly complicated. With White's king still in the centre and so many of Black's pieces actively placed, we feel that Black has at least adequate compensation for the sacrificed material. **17 ... R–N1 18 N×P R–B4 19 Q–K4 N(5)–B3 20 Q–QB4 Q–K2 21 P×N N×P** Material equality has been restored but Black's forces are by far the more active.

White advances P–Q5 and permits Black to exchange pawns, recapturing with the KP

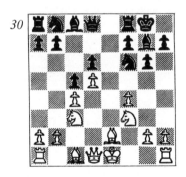

30

Forintos–Gligorić   Ljubljana 1969

The recapture with the KP is, in many ways, unthematic of the Four Pawns Attack, since the idea behind the attack is the advance of the white KP and KBP. Once White has transferred his KP to the Q-file these potentially powerful pawn advances no longer exist, and Black usually experiences less difficulty in reaching a satisfactory position. Many plans are possible for Black in the above position, including the obvious ... R–K1 which stakes an immediate claim to the newly opened file. One of the most popular ideas at Black's disposal is seen after the move **9 ... N–R4** when Black is ready to exchange on ... QB6 and use his knight to defend the K-side. **10 0–0 B×N 11 P×B P–B4** This move prevents the advance of the white KBP. Now White's QB has very little scope. **12 N–N5 N–N2 13 B–B3 N–Q2 14 R–K1** White cannot afford to jump in at K6, because after 14

N-K6 N×N 15 P×N N-B3 16 B-Q5 Q-K2 17 R-K1 N-K5, White will be forced to exchange his Q5 bishop for the knight, leaving Black with the useful light squared bishop which will exert pressure on the forward QBP. **14 ... N-B3 15 R-N1 R-K1 16 R×R+ Q×R 17 R-N2 B-Q2 18 R×P R-N1 19 R×R Q×R** White's extra pawn is of no consequence because his QBPs are doubled and immobile. **20 Q-B2 P-KR3 21 N-R3 Q-K1** and the players soon agreed to a draw.

The golden rules of the Four Pawns Attack

1) White's KP and KBP are dangerous weapons and should be kept under observation at all times.

2) Black must keep control of his ... K4 square, in much the same way as in the Modern Benoni.

3) Black's best route to counterplay often lies in the move ... P-QN4, which sometimes involves the sacrifice of a pawn.

4) If Black is permitted to exchange his QBP for White's QP, the resulting positions tend to favour Black.

5) When White advances P-Q5 it can be dangerous for Black to delay the exchange of his KP (... KP×QP), since if White is allowed to exchange on K6 that square immediately becomes a target for attack.

3 The Sämisch Variation

The Sämisch Variation, **1 P–Q4 N–KB3 2 P–QB4 P–KN3 3 N–QB3 B–N2 4 P–K4 P–Q3 5 P–B3**, brings about one of the basic types of position in the King's Indian Defence.

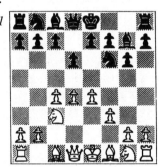

31

Thus far Black has merely declared his intention of playing the King's Indian Defence. White's fifth move, however, is rather more committal. This one move makes an enormous difference to the strategic implications of the position. White voluntarily denies himself the use of his KB3 square for his king's knight in order to reinforce his centre by ensuring that his KP is solidly protected.

The Sämisch Variation is popularly regarded as an aggressive system in which White will castle Q-side and then launch an attack against the black king. Although this does happen in a large percentage of Sämisch games it is nonetheless a dangerous generalisation for White can follow a number of general strategies.

(1) White may castle Q-side, close the centre and launch an attack on the K-side: the most frequent strategy by far.

(2) White may castle Q-side and not close the centre.

(3) White may castle Q-side and launch an offensive on the Q-side.

(4) White may castle K-side and attack on the Q-side.

(5) White may castle K-side and still launch an attack on the enemy king.

Thus almost any general strategy may be used. The plethora of possibilities can be explained by the nature of the position. White's large pawn centre confers on him such flexibility in his choice of plans. In addition, the pawn on KB3 frequently has another major function, apart from supporting the KP, and that is to prop up a K-side onslaught in general and specifically the move P-KN4.

A question which troubles many players is that of whether to leave the centre open or to close it. This largely boils down to a matter of taste and how White wishes to try to exploit his space advantage. If, with White, you want to launch a raging attack against the black king then it goes, almost without saying, that you will close the centre in order to avoid the probably unpleasant repercussions of a sudden central breakthrough by your opponent. This is a cardinal rule of chess, and does not apply solely to the Sämisch Variation or indeed, merely to the King's Indian Defence as a whole. Naturally it is not impossible to have an exception to this rule but they are few and far between. As long as you remember the rule, and also keep an open mind, you will not go far wrong.

However, an all-out attack, or a slow, controlled attack, is not stylistically suitable for all players. Others may simply like to have a little variety. That is where the open centre comes in for those players who would like a less complicated struggle. There are two varieties:

(a) White exchanges in the centre.

(b) White allows Black to exchange on Q4.

If White effects the exchange then the position becomes greatly simplified. White can count on little, if any, advantages unless Black has played . . . P-QB4 but it is a difficult position to lose and White can keep trying to find a way to exploit his extra space right through the endgame.

When White does not himself make the central exchange then there are rather more possibilities for a manoeuvring battle with many pieces on the board. At first sight this type of position may appear to be just as complicated as if White had closed the centre and were preparing for a K-side attack. However, the simplicity decides in several straightforward strategic objectives:

(a) to prevent Black from bursting open the centre, and so freeing his position, by playing . . . P-Q4.

(b) To make as much use as possible for piece manoeuvres of the valuable Q4 and Q5 squares.

(c) If, as a result of (b), Black plays . . . P-QB3, denying White the use of his Q5 square, then the black d-pawn is rather weak. White can then pile up his major pieces on the d-file (still better, they might already be there) and pressurise the backward QP.

If Black has exchanged his QBP for the white QP then the type of position is identical to those discussed in the chapter 'Maroczy Bind Positions' in our companion volume *How to play The Sicilian Defence* and, when you have read what we have to say about this type of position below, you would be well advised to consult that other book for further examples.

Lest it sound that Black is powerless against White's blockading set-up, let us consider Black's possible counterplay. This normally derives from two features of the position,

(1) Four of White's first five moves have been pawn moves and, as a consequence, White will lag behind in development for a few moves. Under some circumstances Black may be able to take advantage of this.

(2) The move 5 P-B3 involves a slight weakening of the dark squares in the centre and on the K-side. This is another feature that the Sämisch has in common with some Maroczy Bind positions in the Sicilian Defence. Again, apart from those below, further examples of how Black can exploit this almost imperceptible weakness can be found in *How to play the Sicilian Defence*.

White castles Q-side and attacks K-side

Ideas for White
(1) Basic attacking:

(a) K-side pawn advance of P-KN4 followed by P-KR4-5 to open the KR-file.

(b) B-KR6 to exchange bishops and weaken the dark squares around Black's king.

(c) N(K2)-KN3-KB5 is often a good manoeuvre to lend weight to the attack.

(2) To use the K4 square (if a pawn exchange on f5 has occurred) for manoeuvring minor pieces into more aggressive positions.

Ideas for Black
(1) The only real idea for Black, apart from warding off immediate threats, is to launch a Q-side counterattack.

White's basic attacking ideas prove successful

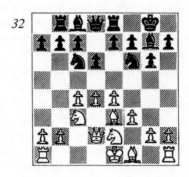

32

Portisch–Pinter   Hungarian Championship 1975

9 P-KR4 P-QR3 10 P-R5! P-QN4 What happens if Black should take the KRP? A thorough analysis is beyond the scope of this book, but see the next position for an example. **11 RP×P BP×P 12 B-R6 B-R1 13 B-N5 R-B1 14 0-0-0 N-QR4 15 N-B4 P-B3** Black's manoeuvres are very slow. There simply is not enough time to defend on the K-side, consolidate the centre *and* counterattack on the Q-side. **16 P-KN4 P-N5 17 N-N1 B×P?** Desperation in this instance, though this can be a useful idea. **18 P×B N×KP 19 Q-R2 N×B 20 N-K6! P-N6 21 N×N** Black resigns.

Deže–Popović   Novi Sad 1975

9 P-KR4 P-QR3 10 P-R5! N×RP 11 B-R6 B×B 12 Q×B P-K4 13 N-Q5 White dominates the KR-file, the centre and has tremendous attacking chances for the pawn. **13 . . . N-B3 14 N(2)-B3 N×QP 15 N×N+ Q×N 16 Q×RP+ K-B1 17 N-Q5 Q-N2 18 Q-R8+ Q-N1 19 Q×Q+ K×Q 20 N-B6+ K-B1 21 N×R K×N 22 R-R8+ K-K2 23 0-0-0** with an enormous advantage for White.

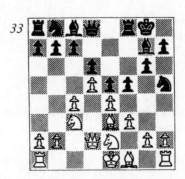

33

Botvinnik-Tal World Championship Match 1961
9 ... N-Q2 9 ... P-B5 may look appealing since it apparently puts a clamp on White's K-side attack, but it has its drawbacks—White's best decision is then probably to attack the base of Black's pawn chain by organizing a timely P-QB5 and launching an attack on the Q-side where he has a great space advantage. **10 KN-K2 P-QR3 11 K-N1 N(2)-B3 12 P×P** It is always difficult to decide whether or when to make this exchange. Here it is well timed as after 12 ... B×P+ 13 K-R1, P-KN4 is a huge threat. **12 ... P×P 13 N-N3** Now Black's K-side is weakened. **13 ... Q-K1** 13 ... P-B5 will not do because of 14 N×N P×B 15 N×N+ Q×N 16 Q×P and White wins both a pawn and the K4 square. **14 B-Q3 N×N 15 P×N P-B4 16 B-R6** softening up the black king's position in the usual manner. **16 ... Q-N3 17 P-KN4 P-N4 18 B×B K×B 19 R-R4 NP×P 20 B-B2** The QN1-KR7 diagonal is far more important than the pawn. **20 ... P-R3 21 R(1)-R1 Q-N4 22 Q×Q+ P×Q 23 R-R6** The exchange of queens has not noticeably reduced White's pressure. **23 ... P×P 24 P×P B×P** Or 24 ... N×NP 25 R-N6+ K-B2 26 R-R7+ K-K1 27 B-R4+. **25 R-N6+ K-B2 26 R-KB1 K-K2 27 R-N7+ K-K1** Or 27 ... R-B2 28 R×R+ K×R+ 29 N-K4, winning a piece. **28 N-K4 N-Q2** If 28 ... N×N, 29 B-R4+ wins immediately. **29 N×QP+ K-Q1 30 R×R+ N×R 31 N×P B-Q2 32 R-B7 K-B2 33 P-Q6+** Black resigns. White wins more material.

Black's counter-attack carries the day

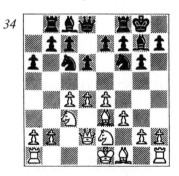

Bagirov-Gufeld U.S.S.R. 1963
9 B-R6 P-QN4 The stage is quickly set. White plays for mate and Black immediately starts his counter-offensive. **10 P-KR4 P-K4 11 B×B K×B 12 P-R5 K-R1!** A good defensive move. Now 13 Q-R6 can be met by 13 ... N-N1. **13 N-Q5 QNP×P 14 RP×P BP×P 15 Q-R6 N-KR4 16 P-KN4** It seems as if White has already established a winning position, but **16 ... R×NP! 17 P×N P-N4** White's attack has been bogged down at the cost of a piece. Black's pieces have excellent freedom of movement.

18 R–KN1 P–N5 19 0–0–0 R×RP 20 N(2)–B4 An ingenious attacking idea but it is not sufficient. **20. . . P×N 21 N×KBP** White now threatens 22 N–N6+. **21 . . . R×N! 22 Q×R P–B6 23 B–B4 R–R6! 24 P×P N–N5 25 K–N1 B–K3!! 26 B×B N–Q6! 27 Q–B7** 27 R×N allows mate in three. **27 . . . Q–QN1+ 28 B–N3 R×B+ 29 K–B2 N–N5+! 30 K×R N–Q4+ 31 K–B2 Q–N7+ 32 K–Q3 Q–N4+** White resigns. The end would be 33 K–B2 Q–K7+ 34 K–N3 Q–QN7+ 35 K–B4 Q–N4 mate.

That was not the most typical example of a counter-attack by Black, but we hope that it may act as inspiration for you.

EXCEPTIONS TO THE MAIN THEME

White castles Q-side and attacks on the Q-side

It may seem odd to a beginner that a recommended scheme for White is to open up the position in front of his king. Surely that is just what Black is trying to do? Yes it is, but often Black simply does not have enough room to manoeuvre his pieces past the central pawn barrier across to the Q-side. By contrast White has oceans of space available on the Q-side it may be much simpler to launch operations there than on the K-side.

Ideas for White

(1) Look for a suitable opportunity to play P–QB5, opening the QB-file or, in some cases, with a view to threatening P–B6.
(2) Attempt to dominate the QB-file if it is open.
(3) Manoeuvre pieces into position to apply pressure to Black's backward QP.

Ideas for Black

(1) Beware of the advance P–QB5(–B6).
(2) Counteract White's pressure along the QB-file (if it is open) or, at the very least, control all the entry squares along it.
(3) Watch for the chance of a tactical counter-thrust to expose the white king.

35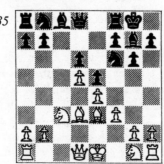

Bobotsov–Gligorić Skopje 1972

9 ... N–R4 10 KN–K2 P–B4 11 Q–Q2 P–B5 12 B–KB2 P–QR3 13 0–0–0 Now we can take stock. Black has sealed up the K-side but White has a large space advantage on the Q-side. **13 ... B–B3 14 K–N1 B–R5** With almost all White's pawns on light squares, it is desirable for Black to exchange dark-squared bishops. **15 B–N1 N–Q2 16 N–B1 N–B4 17 B–QB2 Q–B2** 17 ... P–R4, securing some space on the Q-side, even at the cost of giving White the ... QN4 square, would have been more prudent. **18 P–QN4 N–Q2 19 N–N3 N–N3 20 B–Q3 N–B5 21 B×N Q×B 22 N–R4 Q–B2 23 R–QB1** White is the first to get a rook to the QB-file, something Black never succeeds in achieving. **23 ... Q–Q1 24 N–N6 R–N1 25 B–B2 B×B** Retreating the bishop, with a view to placing it on ... Q1, to cover one QB-file entry square, might have been better. **26 Q×B N–B3 27 P–QR4 B–Q2 28 R–B3 P–N4 29 R(1)–QB1 B–K1 30 K–N2 N–Q2** Note how difficult it is for Black to manoeuvre and how easy it seems for White to increase his pressure. **31 P–R5 N–B3 32 N–B8!** The threat of 33 Q–R7 wins material. **32 ... P–N3 33 N×NP B–N4 34 R–B7 N–K1 35 R–B8 R×R 36 N×R P–N5 37 N–R7 B–Q2 38 N–B6 Q–N4 39 P–N5** The decisive break. **39 ... RP×P 40 P–R6 N–B3 41 P–R7 R–R1 42 R–B2 Q–N2 43 Q–N6 N–K1 44 N(3)–R5** Black resigns. Nothing can be done about the threat of Q–N7 or, if White prefers, Q–N8.

White castles K-side and attacks on the Q-side

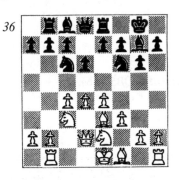

Timman–Marović Amsterdam 1973

9 ... P–QR4?! Now the black rook on QN1 has no scope. 9 ... P–QR3 would have given better chances. **10 P–KN3** Reinforcing White's already massive centre. **10 ... N–Q2 11 B–N2 P–K4 12 P–Q5 N–K2 13 0–0 P–N3 14 P–QR3 B–QR3 15 P–N3 P–KB4 16 N–N5!** A useful idea, enabling White to proceed with P–QN4, which is worth remembering. **16 ... N–KB3 17 K–R1 R–KB1 18 N(K2)–B3 N–R4 19 B–B2 K–R1 20 P–QN4** Now White's Q-side play will take some stopping. **20 ... RP×P**

21 RP×P N-N1 22 R-R1 B-R3 23 Q-K2 B×N 24 N×B N(R4)-B3 25 P-B5 NP×P 26 NP×P N-K1 27 P-B6 Fixing a permanent target on QB7 which can subsequently be attacked along the seventh rank. **27 ... P-B5 28 R-R7 P×P 29 P×P N(N1)-B3 30 B-R3 N-R4 31 B-N4 R-B2 32 K-N2 Q-N4 33 R-N7 R-R1 34 R-KR1 R-Q1** Black can undertake nothing constructive. **35 B-N6! N(K1)-B3 36 R×P N×B 37 R×R** and Black lost on time, just in time, e.g. 37 ... N×NP 38 B×R N-K6+ 39 Q×N! and White wins easily.

White castles K-side and attacks on the K-side

37

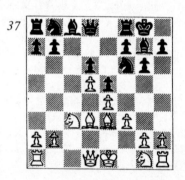

Portisch-Donner   Wijk aan Zee 1975

9 ... N-K1 One of the two principal methods of freeing the advance of the KBP. 9 ... N-R4 is the other. **10 Q-Q2!** Black was threatening 10 ... B-R3! 11 B×B Q-R5+, exchanging off his poor dark-squared bishop. **10 ... P-B4 11 P×P P×P 12 KN-K2 N-Q2 13 0-0 N-B4?!** It is very dangerous for Black to move his pieces over to the Q-side when White has such a piece barrage aimed at the K-side. **14 B-QB2 P-QR4 15 P-B4 P×P** 15 ... P-K5, allowing White complete control of his Q4 square and a potential break with P-KN4 would have been as bad. **16 N×P B-K4 17 QR-K1 Q-B3 18 N-R3 P-N3 19 B-KN5 Q-N3 20 B-B4 B-KB3 21 R-B3 K-R1 22 R-N3 Q-R4 23 B-Q1 Q-R5 24 N-KN5** Now the threat is 25 N-B7+. **24 ... N-K5 25 N(N5)×N P×N 26 N×P** and Black resigned. He is only a pawn down but his position is hopeless.

Golden rules

(1) With such a wide choice of strategic plans to choose from, White should ensure that he sticks to one and must avoid changing horses in midstream.

(2) White is at liberty either to close the centre or to open it. Black choices are more restricted and, if the centre is closed, he must beware of advancing his KBP to B5 if this will allow White to make use of his K4 square.

(3) Both sides must bear in mind the most common blockading and sacrificial ideas:

(a) ... P-KR4 by Black, in reply to P-KN4 by White, as long as the KRP is protected by a knight on KB3.

(b) the temporary piece sacrifice ... B-KR3, followed by ... Q-KR5+, regaining the piece and thereby effecting the exchange of Black's bad bishop for White's good bishop.

(c) White's N-KB5 putting intolerable pressure on the black K-side.

(d) an automatic advance of White's K-side pawns (KN and KR) to burst open the defences around the opposing king.

(4) Endgames favour White because of his space advantage which makes it easy for him to switch play from one side of the board to the other.

4 The Averbakh System

The Averbakh System, popularised by the Russian grandmaster Yuri Averbakh in the 1950's arises from the following move order: **1 P–Q4 N–KB3 2 P–QB4 P–KN3 3 N–QB3 B–N2 4 P–K4 P–Q3 5 B–K2 0–0 6 B–N5**

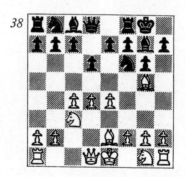

At first sight it may appear that there is nothing very significant about this move order and that the play will closely resemble the variations considered in Chapter 6 (Petrosian System) and Chapter 5 (Classical System). Nonetheless there are important differences.

In the Petrosian System White does not play B–KN5 until Black has played ... P–K4. In the Averbakh System White plays B–KN5 before Black has decided whether to strike back in the centre by ... P–K4 or ... P–B4. In practice Black usually plays ... P–B4 rather than ... P–K4 leading to positions radically different from those arising in the Petrosian System.

In the Classical System, in which White plays 6 N–B3 instead of 6 B–N5 Black's almost invariable reply is 6 ... P–K4. But against 6 B–N5 the immediate 6 ... P–K4 is a blunder. White continues 7 PXP! PXP 8 QXQ RXQ and gains a decisive material advantage by either 9 N–Q5 or 9 BXN BXB 10 N–Q5. This is a very important trap which has claimed many victims. If you play the Averbakh System regularly as White you will be unlucky if you do not pick up a few 'free' points in this way.

Since the immediate 6 ... P-K4 is unplayable Black usually opts for the alternative central break 6 ... P-B4 and most of this chapter will be devoted to that move. At the end of the chapter we consider briefly the main alternatives 6 ... P-KR3 and 6 ... QN-Q2 planning 7 ... P-K4.

After 6 ... P-B4 White almost invariably replies 7 P-Q5. The alternatives 7 PXP Q-R4! and 7 N-B3 PXP lead to 'Maroczy Bind' positions similar to those discussed in Chapter 2 of *How to Play the Sicilian Defence*. White's bishop is not well placed on KN5 in such positions and so Black should have no difficulty in equalizing.

After (1 P-Q4 N-KB3 2 P-QB4 P-KN3 3 N-QB3 B-N2 4 P-K4 P-Q3 5 B-K2 0-0 6 B-N5) **6 ... P-B4 7 P-Q5** we reach the basic position in the Averbakh System.

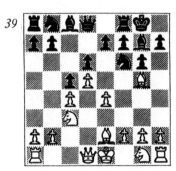

39

Ideas for White
As in many variations of the King's Indian Defence, White has a space advantage and his correct strategy depends on how Black seeks to counteract this. In general White should try to prevent Black obtaining any counterplay and rely on his long term space advantage.

Ideas for Black
1. Black blocks the centre by ... P-K4. This is not a good idea since White's space advantage makes it easier for him to organise an attack on the kingside than it is for Black to organise counterplay either on the queenside or the kingside.
2. Black seeks immediate counterplay on the queenside, without playing ... P-K3. This is quite a promising idea and it is certainly logical since by playing B-KN5 White has slightly weakened his queenside.
3. Black strikes back in the centre by ... P-K3. This is in practice Black's most popular plan. White usually allows Black to play ... PXQP and he then has the choice between two recaptures. BPXP leads to Modern Benoni positions which are outside the scope of this book. KPXP leads to

pure Averbakh Systems. White's strategy is then to head for endgames which generally favour White. Black should try to obtain counterchances in the middlegame.

4. Unless White is careful Black can rapidly build up an overwhelming queenside attack by such moves as ... Q-R4, ... P-QR3 and ... P-QN4. White's correct antidote is to answer ... Q-R4 by B-Q2 and ... P-QR3 by P-QR4. Black then has little option but to abandon the idea of immediate queenside play and revert to a central break by ... P-K3 leading to positions similar to those considered in the next paragraph.

Black blocks the centre by ... P-K4

Averbakh–Panno   USSR–Argentina 1954

1 P-Q4 N-KB3 2 P-QB4 P-KN3 3 N-QB3 B-N2 4 P-K4 P-Q3 5 B-K2 0-0 6 B-N5 P-B4 7 P-Q5 P-QR3 8 P-QR4 Q-R4 9 B-Q2 P-K4?

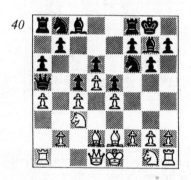

40

10 P-KN4! Now that the centre is blocked White does not have to worry too much about the safety of his own king. He is able to exploit his space advantage by launching a direct assault on his opponent's king. **10 ... N-K1 11 P-R4 P-B4 12 P-R5 P-B5** Black decides to block the position still further in the hope of establishing an impregnable fortress on the kingside. He thus condemns himself to passive (and ultimately unavailing) defence. **13 P-N5! R-B2 14 B-N4** The exchange of the light squared bishops increased the strength of White's attack. **14 ... Q-Q1 15 BXB QXB 16 N-B3 B-B1 17 K-K2!** White clears the way for the transfer of his pieces to the kingside. **17 ... R-N2 18 R-R4 N-Q2 19 PXP PXP 20 Q-R1 B-K2 21 R-R8+ K-B2 22 Q-R6 N-B1 23 R-R1 R-QN1**

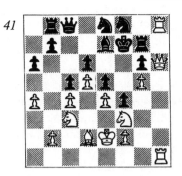

41

24 B×P! So Black's fortress is not impregnable after all! If 24 . . . P×B 25 R-R4 is decisive. **24 . . . Q-B2 25 Q-R2 N-Q2 26 Q-R3 N-B1 27 R×N+ K×R 28 Q-K6 R-N1 29 N-R4 B-Q1 30 N×P+ K-N2 31 N×P 1-0.**

Black never obtained the ghost of a counterattack after closing the centre and White was able to build up a massive attack at his leisure.

Black seeks immediate counterplay on the queenside

Kristinsson–Olafsson   Reykjavik 1966
From Diagram 39 Play continued **7 . . . P-QR3 8 P-QR4!** An essential precaution. If White unguardedly continues his development by 8 N-B3? then 8 . . . P-N4! is very strong, e.g. 9 P×P P×P 10 B×P (or 10 N×P N×P) 10 . . . N×P! 11 N×N Q-R4+ is good for Black. **8 . . . P-R3 9 B-R4?** The bishop is out of play here as Black promptly demonstrates. Correct was 9 B-B4 when play might continue 9 . . . Q-R4. (The immediate 9 . . . P-K3 loses a pawn after 10 P×P and 11 B×QP) 10 B-Q2 P-K3 leading to the same position as Diagram 48 with the unimportant difference that Black has a pawn on KR3 rather than KR2. **9 . . . Q-R4 10 Q-Q2** Black threatened 10 . . . N×KP and after his inaccurate ninth move White was no longer able to prevent this by B-Q2. **10 . . . QN-Q2 11 N-B3?** The ugly 11 R-R3, preventing Black's next move was comparatively best.

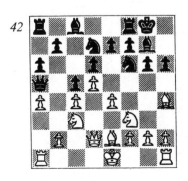

42

11 ... P-QN4! Black was now well on top. Play continued **12 BP×P P×P 13 B×P N×KP!** **14 N×N Q×B!** and Black gained a decisive material advantage.

This extract shows what can go wrong for White. Let us see how he should answer Black's plan.

From Diagram 39 play could continue **7 ... P-QR3** If 7 ... Q-R4 8 B-Q2!. **8 P-QR4 Q-R4** This is the normal move. 8 ... P-KR3 (played in the previous extract) 9 B-B4! Q-R4 10 B-Q2 P-KR3 leads to more or less the same position. **9 B-Q2!** This loss of a tempo is well justified. The bishop has already served a useful purpose on KN5 by inducing ... P-B4 rather than P-K4. Moreover Black will eventually have to move his queen from the exposed square QR4 and so each player will have lost a tempo. **9 ... P-K3** We have now reached a position similar to Diagram 44 considered in the next section.

Black strikes back in the centre by 7 ... P-K3

7 ... P-K3, striking back at White's centre is in practice Black's most popular move.

43

8 P×P now gives Black a comfortable game after 8 ... B×P! (The recapture 8 ... P×P is not so good as it allows the promising positional pawn sacrifice 9 P-K5!). Black's lead in development more than compensates for the weakness of his queen's pawn.

After 8 N-B3 (8 Q-Q2 is also often played and leads to similar positions) 8 ... P×P we reach another parting of the ways.

44

White can recapture the queen's pawn in three ways:

(a) 9 N×P is rarely played. It leads to positions similar to those reached after 8 P×P B×P. The activity of Black's pieces outweigh the importance of his weak queen's pawn.

(b) 9 BP×P transposes into a position from the Modern Benoni Defence which more often arises from the move order 1 P-Q4 N-KB3 2 P-QB4 P-B4 3 P-Q5 P-K3 4 N-QB3 P×P 5 P×P P-Q3 6 P-K4 P-KN3 7 B-K2 B-N2 8 B-N5 0-0 9 N-B3. The detailed treatment of the Modern Benoni lies beyond the scope of this book. Suffice it to say that a typical continuation is 9 ... P-KR3 10 B-R4 P-KN4 11 B-N3 N-R4 12 N-Q2 N×B 13 RP×N N-Q2 14 N-B4 Q-K2 with equality. Black's slight weakness on the white squares is counterbalanced by White's slight weakness on the black squares.

(c) 9 KP×P is White's most promising continuation. By recapturing with his king's pawn White gives up any chance of a later breakthrough in the centre by P-K5. But he also deprives Black of the opportunity of attacking White's king's pawn. White has a slight space advantage and Black's queen's pawn could become weak. Experience has shown that endgames arising from this variation tend to favour White. White should therefore be happy to allow exchanges (especially on the open king's file) while Black should seek counterplay in the middlegame.

Here are two examples:

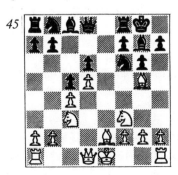

45

Uhlmann-Gligorić   Hastings 1970/71
From Diagram 45 play continued **9 . . . R-K1**. This move looks natural
but it is based on a faulty idea. Black hopes that the ultimate exchange of
major pieces on the king's file will lead to an ending which it is easy for
him to draw. In fact the ending turns out to be very uncomfortable for
Black. A better plan for Black, based on the moves . . . P-QR3, . . . Q-B2,
. . . B-N5, . . . N-K1 and . . . P-B4 is demonstrated in the next extract.
10 Q-Q2 B-N5 If Black tries to avoid surrendering the bishop by
playing 10 . . . B-B4 White can drive the bishop back by 11 N-KR4.
11 0-0 QN-Q2 12 P-KR3 B×N 13 B×B P-QR3 14 P-QR4 White snuffs
out Black's hopes of obtaining queenside counterplay by . . . P-QN4. **14 . . .
Q-K2 15 QR-K1 Q-B1 16 B-Q1 R×R 17 R×R R-K1 18 R×R Q×R 19
B-B4 Q-K2 20 Q-K2 K-B1 21 Q×Q+ K×Q**

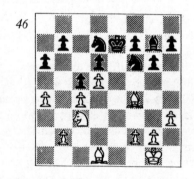

46

Black has now reached the ending he was aiming for, but his troubles
have only just begun. The way in which White gradually exploits his small
advantages (bishop pair, more space, weak Black queen's pawn) is very
instructive. **22 P-R5!** This prevents Black from bolstering up his queenside
by . . . P-QN3 and so prepares the way for the eventual break P-QN4.
22 . . . N-K1 23 B-Q2 It would be a bad positional mistake to allow the
white queen's bishop pawns to be doubled by . . . B×N. **23 . . . P-R4 24
K-B1 B-Q5 25 P-QN3 N-N2 26 B-B2 N-K1 27 N-K2 B-N7 28 P-B3
N-N2 29 K-B2 B-B3 30 N-B3 B-Q5+ 31 K-K2 P-B4 32 P-B4 N-K1
33 B-Q3 B×N?** This exchange makes matters worse for Black. It would
have been better to have carried on marking time by 33 . . . N-N2 though
White would still have had good prospects after 34 N-Q1 planning N-K3
and P-KN4. **34 B×B N(K1)-B3 35 B-K1 K-B2 36 K-K3 K-K2 37 B-QB2·
K-B2**

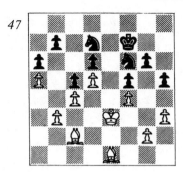

47

The manoeuvring phase of the game is over. White is ready to open up the position for his bishop pair by advances on both wings. Note how the absence of major pieces has meant that Black has been forced to sit back idly while White prepared these advances at his leisure. **38 P–QN4! P×P 39 B×NP N–B4 40 K–Q4 N(B3)–Q2 41 B–Q1 K–K2 42 P–N4!** For the time being White is unable to make further progress on the queenside. So he switches his attention to the other wing. The advantage of the bishop pair is always accentuated when there is play on both wings. **42 . . . RP×P 43 P×P K–B3 44 K–K3 P–N3 45 NP×P KNP×P 46 B×N!** The bishop pair has served its purpose and it is now time for White to cash in his advantage. **46 . . . N×B** Pawn recaptures were no better, e.g. 46 . . . NP×P 47 B–R4 N–N1–if 47 . . . N–B1 48 B–B6 followed by 49 B–N7 wins the rook's pawn–48 K–B3 and the white king penetrates Black's kingside. **47 P×P** White has now won a vital pawn and the rest is easy. **47 . . . P–R4 48 B–B2 K–K2 49 K–Q2 K–Q1 50 B×P N–R5 51 P–N7 K–B2 52 B–B8 N–B4 53 P–B5 N–K5+ 54 K–B2 K–N1 55 K–N3 N–Q7+ 56 K–R4 N×P 57 P–B6 N–K4 58 K×P Black resigned**.

Now let us look at a more effective way for Black to treat this system.

Lombard–Gligorić   Siegen Olympiad 1970

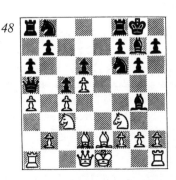

48

After eleven moves the position in Diagram 48 was reached. The position differs in detail from Diagram 45 but the strategic features are the same. Play continued **12 0-0 Q-B2 13 P-R3 B×N 14 B×B QN-Q2 15 Q-B2 N-K1!** Black rejects the routine 15 . . . R-K1 and plays to gain space on the kingside instead. **16 B-K2 P-B4 17 P-B4 B-Q5+ 18 K-R2 N-N2 19 B-B3 QR-K1 20 N-K2** Better was 20 QR-K1 trying to exchange all major pieces as in the previous game. **20 . . . B-K6!** Black begins to seize the initiative. **21 B-K1 N-B3 22 R-R3 Q-K2 23 R-Q3 P-KN4** Black should have prepared this move by 23 . . . P-R3 **24 P×P B×P 25 B-Q2?** White should have exploited Black's inaccuracy on move 23 by 25 B-N3 gaining control of the square KB4. **25 . . . Q-K4+ 26 P-N3?** A mistake but Black already had the advantage.

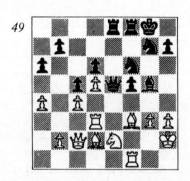

49

26 . . . Q×N+! 27 K-N1 If 27 B×Q R×Bch 28 K-N1 N-K5 29 R-Q1 R(B1)-K1 and White is completely tied down. **27 . . . Q-K4 28 B×B Q×P+** Black has won a pawn and went on to win the game in 42 moves.

Black plays 6 . . . P-KR3

6 . . . P-KR3 is a natural reply to 6 B-N5. The object is to force White's bishop to commit itself before Black decides how to react in the centre.

At one time the move 6 . . . P-KR3 was as popular as 6 . . . P-B4 which we have so far been considering. But it is now considered dubious after 7 B-K3! The fact that 7 B-K3 is White's best move can readily be seen from a brief examination of the alternatives.

(a) 7 B×N? This is clearly bad as White surrenders the two bishops without compensation. Black stands well after either 7 . . . B×B or 7 . . . P×B planning to undermine White's centre by . . . P-KB4.

(b) 7 B-R4. This looks a natural retreat but it is in fact a mistake. After 7 . . . P-B4 8 P-Q5 P-QR3 9 P-QR4 Q-R4 the game transposes into

Kristinsson–Olafsson (see page 35). Black has a dangerous initiative on the queenside.

(c) 7 B–B4 N–B3! and Black stands well after either 8 P–Q5 P–K4! or 8 N–B3 NxQP! After 7 B–K3 Black has two alternatives neither of which is entirely satisfactory.

(1) 7 ... P–B4 8 P–K5! This is the new move which has cast doubt on Black's whole system commencing 6 ... P–KR3. Previously the normal continuation was 8 P–Q5 (8 PxP Q–R4! is not dangerous for Black) 8 ... P–K3 transposing into positions similar to those considered on page 36.

After 8 P–K5 the game Kierzek–Margononi, Dortmund 1978, continued, 8 ... KN–Q2 (8 ... QPxP 9 PxKP QxQ+ 10 RxQ N–N5 11 BxBP NxKP 12 N–Q5 is also bad for Black while 8 ... BPxP? simply loses a piece after 9 PxN. Note that if the White bishop was still on KN5 this last variation would not work in view of 9 ... PxP! attacking the bishop)–9 KPxP KPxP 10 N–B3 N–B3 11 Q–Q2

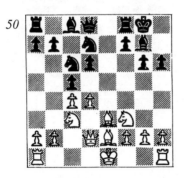

50

White stands well since he has an advantage in space and Black's queen pawn is weak.

(2) 7 ... P–K4 8 P–Q5 QN–Q2. 8 ... P–B3 intending to open the queen's bishop's file is also playable though still not good enough for full equality. 9 Q–Q2!

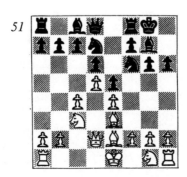

51

Now we see one of the disadvantages of 6 . . . P–KR3. Black is forced to waste a tempo defending the KRP and so White's kingside attack gains momentum. Taylor–Biyiasas, USA 1977, continued **9 . . . K–R2** The immediate 9 . . . P–KR4 was better. **10 P–KN4 N–B4 11 P–B3 P–QR4 12 P–KR4 P–R4** White threatened 13 P–R5 leaving Black with the unpleasant alternative of allowing the KR file to be opened or playing 13 . . . P–KN4 and conceding White a glorious square for a knight on KB5. If Black ever captured that knight, White would play KPXN obtaining an equally good outpost on K4. **13 N–R3!** PXP? comparatively best was 13 . . . R–R1 14 N–N5+ K–N1. **14 N–N5+ K–N1 15 O–O–O**

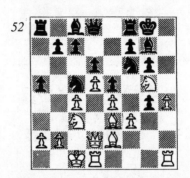

52

Black's kingside is like a pin-cushion and the pricks soon proved fatal. **15 . . . PXP 16 BXP N–R4 17 R(Q1)–N1 P–B4 18 N–K6?** 18 BXN PXB 19 Q–K2 was more accurate since Black could now have put up considerable resistance by 18 . . . NXN 19 PXN P–B5! **18 . . . BXN? 19 PXB P–B5 20 QBXN PXB 21 N–Q5 N–N6 22 P–K7 Q–Q3 23 PXR=Q+** Black resigned.

Black plays 6 . . . QN–Q2 and 7 . . . P–K4

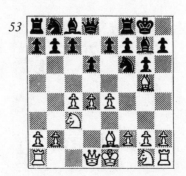

53

We have seen that 6 . . . P-K4? is a blunder losing to 7 P×P P×P 8 Q×Q R×Q 9 B×N (or 9 N-Q5) 9 . . . B×B 10 N-Q5. The attempt to prepare . . . P-K4 by 6 . . . P-KR3 also has drawbacks (see page 40). However there is one move order by which Black can get in . . . P-K4 in satisfactory circumstances.

From Diagram 53 play can continue 6 . . . QN-Q2 7 Q-Q2. 7 N-B3 P-K4 8 P-Q5 transposes into the Petrosian System considered on page 55 while 7 N-B3 P-K4 8 Q-Q2 transposes back into the text. 7 . . . P-K4

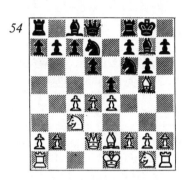

White must now decide whether to close the centre.
(a) 8 N-B3 P-B3 9 0-0 P×P 10 N×P N-B4 11 P-B3? Correct is 11 Q-B4 leading to an equal position after 11 . . . Q-K2 12 QR-Q1 Q-K4!

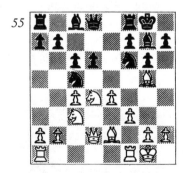

11 . . . KN×P! Black now wins a pawn, e.g. 12 P×N B×N+ 13 Q×B Q×B 14 Q×P Q-K6+ 15 K-R1 N×P. Grandmaster Geller must have a particular affection for this trap. It once netted him two points in the same tournament (against Holm and Adamski at Lugano 1968).
(b) 8 P-Q5 More promising than 8 N-B3

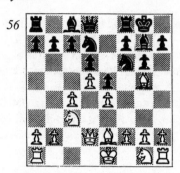

56

The only difference between Diagram 56 and Diagram 70 (Petrosian System, page 56) is that White has played Q–Q2 instead of N–KB3. The advantage for White is that Black cannot (at least for the time being) break the pin on his king's knight by ... P–KR3 and so has difficulty getting in the thematic ... P–KB4. If Black ever does manage to play ... P–KR3 White may be able to reply B–K3 (which is dubious in the Petrosian System because of the reply ... N–KN5) and Black's KRP is uncomfortably placed. To compensate for this, after Black's normal move 8 ... N–B4 White has no entirely satisfactory way of defending his KP and is forced to resort to a rather artificial way of completing his development. Theory at present considers White stands rather better but the position is complex and the better player is likely to win. Here are a few examples of play after 8 ... N–B4.

(a) 9 P–QN4(?) QN×P 10 N×N N×N 11 B×Q N×Q 12 B×P P–K5 13 R–B1 P–K6 with great complications in which Black certainly stands no worse.

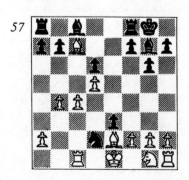

57

Lukacs–Toth, Hungarian Championship 1971 ended unnecessarily abruptly after weak play by White. **14 P–B3?** Better was 14 B×P. **14 ...**

B–N7 15 R–B2 B–K4 16 P–B5? B–B4 17 R–B1 KR–B1 18 P–N4 B–Q2
White resigned.

(b) Hort–Savon, Havanna 1967. **9 P–B3** White's position now becomes a
little congested since he cannot develop his king's knight on either of the
two natural squares K2 or KB3. **9 . . . P–B3** If 9 . . . P–KR3 White plays
10 B–K3 rather than 10 B×P? or 10 B–R4? both of which allow the
riposte 10 . . . KN×P! **10 P–QN4 N–R3 11 P–QR3 P×P 12 BP×P P–KR3**.
This weakening move is now justified since Black has time to work up
enough counterplay before White steamrollers him on the kingside. 13
B–K3 Again 13 B×P and 13 B–R4 fail to 13 . . . KN×P. **13 . . . N–R4 14
B–Q3 P–B4 15 KN–K2 N–B5**

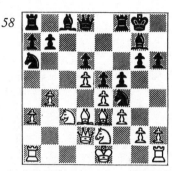

58

A very complex position has arisen in which chances are about level.

(c) Olafsson–Savon, Moscow 1971. **9 . . . B–B3** This is an unnatural square for
the bishop but at least it allows White to complete his development. 9 . . .
P–QR3 10 P–KR4 10 R–Q1 preventing 10 . . . P–B3 may be better. 10 . . .
P–B3 11 KN–K2 P–QN4 12 QP×P Black obtains excellent compensation
for the pawn after 12 BP×P P×NP 13 N×NP R–N1 **12 . . . P×P 13 N–Q5**.

White stands a little better but Black has plenty of practical chances of
outplaying his opponent in the complications.

5 The Classical System

The Classical Variation typifies the King's Indian strategies for both White and Black. The basic pawn structure consists of a locked centre and a fluid situation on the wings, with the inevitable result that White will attack on the Q-side while Black will counter on the K-side. These strategies will be better understood after studying the following diagram.

59
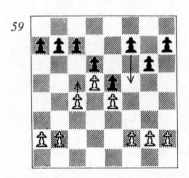

White's Q-side attack will be based on the advance of the QBP to B5, possibly supported by the neighbouring QNP which often moves to QN4. Once White achieves P-QB5 Black must lose some ground on the Q-side: either he captures ... QP×P, leaving White with a strong pawn on Q5, or Black permits the exchange of White's QBP on Q6, when the QB-file is opened and Black's central pawn chain has a potentially vulnerable base at ... Q3.

Black's K-side action is inaugurated by the thrust ... P-KB4. Black will then be in a position to advance on the K-side still further, with ... P-KB5 and ... P-KN4-N5, or he can create piece play along the KB-file by exchanging pawns on ... K5. When White exchanges pawns, by KP×KBP, Black normally recaptures with the KNP even though this appears to weaken him on the K-side. In fact, after recapturing with the KNP, Black can often launch an attack down the KN-file, using his pawn duo at ... K4 and ... KB4 to support his minor pieces and to make White's defensive task more difficult.

Before we enter a detailed discussion of all aspects of the two strategies, let us first examine two games which illustrate how these strategies may work out in practice.

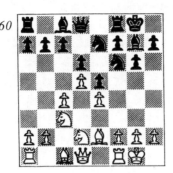

60

Bukić–Marjanović   Yugoslavia 1970

9 ... N–Q2 Preparing for ... P–KB4 while keeping an eye on the ... QB4 square. **10 P–QN4 P–KB4 11 P–B3 N–KB3** It is necessary for Black to lose time by moving his KB3 knight out of the way and then moving it back, since the knight will be an important attacking piece on the K-side if Black's plans come to fruition. **12 P–B5 P–B5 13 N–B4 P–KN4** Both sides attack vigorously on the wings where they hold the advantage. **14 P–QR4 N–N3 15 B–R3** Increasing the pressure on Q6. **15 ... R–B2 16 P–N5 B–B1 17 P–R5**

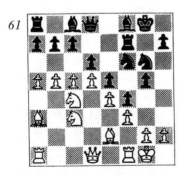

61

It is not difficult to see that White's Q-side attack has made considerably more progress than his opponent's action on the K-wing. **17 ... P–N3** After 17 ... PXP White continues his Q-side attack with 18 P–N6! RPXP 19 PXP PXP 20 Q–N3, for example 20 ... P–N5 21 NXNP R–N1 22 P–Q6, with an enormous advantage on the Q-side. **18 BPXNP BPXP 19 PXP PXP** Now Black has weak pawns at ... QN3 and ... Q3. **20 N–R2!** Taking advantage of Black's weakness at ...QB3. **20 ... P–N5 21 N–N4 P–N6 22 N–B6 P×P+ 23 K×P Q–B2 24 B–N4 R×R 25 Q×R** Now White's domination of the Q-side is complete and Black's position quickly crumbles. **25 ... R–N2 26 Q–R8 N–R5 27 R–B2 R–N6 28 B–B1 Q–KN2 29 Q×B Q–R3 30 K–N1 N×BP+ 31 R×N N–N5 32 Q–K6+** Black Resigned. His K-side counterattack was just a little bit too slow.

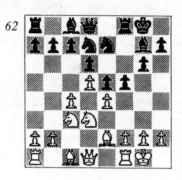

62

Najdorf–Gligorić   Mar Del Plata 1953

Here we see a similar Q-side vs K-side struggle, but this time Black's attack comes first. **11 P–B3 P–B5 12 B–Q2 N–KB3 13 P–QN4 P–KN4 14 P–B5 P–KR4 15 N–B2 N–N3 16 R–B1** In readiness for the opening of the QB-file. **16 ... R–B2 17 P×P P×P 18 P–QR4 B–B1!** A multipurpose move. The second rank is cleared for use by Black's rooks and queen. The bishop overprotects the vulnerable pawn at ... Q3, thereby freeing the queen for its attacking duties on the K-side. Finally, the bishop on KB1 protects the black king from checks along the rank in case White manages to infiltrate to the end of the QB-file. **19 P–R5 R–N2 20 P–R3 N–R1!** Preparing for the advance of the KNP. **21 N–N5 P–N5**

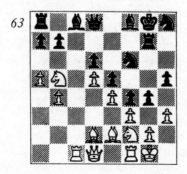

63

Black's attack has made much more progress than in the previous example whereas White has nothing much to show for his Q-side excursion. There is no way to increase the pressure on Black's QP and White's rook can do little on the QB-file. **22 BP×P P×P 23 P×P P-R3 24 N-QR3** Aiming for QN6 via QB4. **24 ... B-Q2 25 N-B4 R-B1 26 N-N6 R×R 27 B×R B-K1** But now the knight, which has reached its target square, can do black no harm. **28 B-R3 N-B2 29 Q-B2 N-R3 30 P-KN5** Decoying the black rook off the second rank, since the pawn was doomed anyway. **30 ... R×P 31 R-B1** White could prolong the game by exchanging queens on QB8 but then a black knight would invade ... KN5 and ... K6 to decisive effect. **31 ... R-N6! 32 B-N2 N(B3)-N5 33 N×N N×N 34 B×N R×B 35 Q-B2 B-N3 36 R-B4 Q-K2 37 B-B3 Q-R2 38 Q-K2 R-R5 39 K-B2 P-B6!** Smashing open the last vestige of cover shielding White's king. **40 Q-K3 R-B5 41 P×P Q-R7+ 42 K-K1 Q-R8+ 43 K-K2 B-R4 44 K-Q2 R×BP!** Correctly judging that White's queen cannot cause any problems. **45 Q-N5+ B-N2 46 K-B2 R-B7+ 47 B-Q2 Q-Q8+ 48 K-B3 Q-QR8+** White Resigns. Mate is inevitable.

Gligorić's handling of the King's Indian demonstrates an understanding of the opening that is second to none in international chess. Whether playing the white side or the black, Gligorić is equally at home. A collection of his King's Indian games would, in themselves, form an excellent text book on this opening and the reader is well advised to study any game in which Gligorić plays the King's Indian with either colour.

Now that we have seen how each player's strategy can work out in practice we shall take a closer look at various aspects of White's Q-side attack and Black's K-side counterattack.

White's Basic Strategy

To attack forcefully on the Q-side, which means:

1) Being aware of the possibilities at Black's disposal to slow down White's attack.

2) Ensuring that every move is directed towards furthering the attack or holding back Black's counterplay on the opposite wing.

3) To strengthen his position.

4) Ultimately, to squash Black on the Q-side.

Black's Basic Strategy

To attack forcefully on the K-side, which means:

1) Advancing the KBP and KNP and then filling the space behind these pawns with pieces which can carry out the final attack.

2) Ensuring that no time is lost in prosecuting the attack.

3) Being on the lookout for ways to slow down White's Q-side advance.

4) To strengthen his position.

5) Ultimately, to smash open White's king defences.

Ideas for Black on the Q-side

Black has two important ideas for slowing down White's Q-side advance:
The move . . . P-QR4, which reduces the effect of White's P-QN4; and the
move . . . P-QB4, which prevents the advance of the QBP to QB5.

Black Plays . . . P-QR4

This move is often played in conjunction with . . . N-QB4, since Black's
knight would otherwise be vulnerable to attack from the advance of White's
QNP. It is interesting to note that in many positions Black can afford to
play . . . N-B4 before . . . P-QR4, since the move . . . N-B4 often threatens
the white KP, and only when White has defended the KP need Black play
. . . P-QR4.

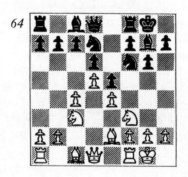

Black can safely play 8 . . . N-B4, since 9 P-QN4?? loses the KP. White
must spend his next move defending this pawn and then 9 . . . P-QR4 will
hold back the White QNP.

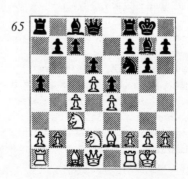

Here is an example of Black playing ... P-QR4 without a subsequent ... N-QB4. **10 P-QR3** Still aiming for P-QN4. **10 ... N-Q2 11 R-N1 P-KB4** While White has been consuming time on the Q-side Black has reacted promptly on the other wing. **12 P-QN4 P-N3 13 N-N3 RPXP 14 RPXP PXP 15 NXP** White's Q-side pawns do not look so impressive now that the supporting QRP and KP have been exchanged off. If White advances P-QB5 he will be left with a weak QP.

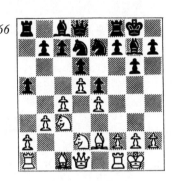

66

Mikhailchishin-Braga   Mexico City 1977

In this position Black has just played ... N-Q2, en route for ... QB4, and so White takes steps to undermine the knight when it gets there. **11 B-R3 N-B4 12 P-QN4 PXP 13 BXP N-R3 14 B-R3 P-N3 15 N-N3** Staking a firm claim on the QB5 square. **15 ... P-KB4 16 B-B1** Intending P-QR4-R5. **16 ... N-B4 17 NXN NPXN?** This recapture cedes too much ground on the Q-side. 17 ... QPXN was better. **18 P-QR4 K-R1 19 B-Q2 N-N1** This is a fairly common manoeuvre, designed to regroup the knight from ... K2 to ... KB3. **20 P-R5 B-KR3 21 PXBP BXP** After 21 ... PXBP 22 BXB NXB, Black's knight is misplaced because it no longer has the possibility of moving to ... KB4. **22 P-R6 B-Q2 23 P-R7 Q-B1 24 Q-B2 BXB 25 QXB N-K2 26 B-Q3 R-B5 27 KR-N1 B-B4 28 N-K2 BXB 29 QXB R-B1 30 R-N2 N-B4 31 P-B4 R-K1 32 PXP RXKP 33 QR-N1 R-K6??** An oversight, but even after 33 ... Q-B1 34 R-N8 R-K1 35 RXR(K8) QXR 36 R-N7, Black would have very little hope of survival. **34 QXR!** Black Resigns because of 34 ... NXQ 35 R-N8, winning. The ultimate in Q-side advances—White forces the promotion of the QRP.

Black Plays ... P-QB4

The move ... P-QB4 leaves the centre completely locked, with White having a pawn wedge on QB4, Q5 and K4 against Black's somewhat more restrictive formation on ... QB4, ... Q3 and ... K4.

67

Petrosian–Lutikov   U.S.S.R. Championship 1959
This position is not quite typical inasmuch as White has normally castled
at an earlier stage, but Petrosian's subsequent play is worthy of study as an
example of how White can expand on the Q-side even after Black plays the
resilient looking . . . P-QB4. **10 N-Q2 B-Q2 11 N-N5!** The logical way to
take advantage of Black's somewhat inflexible structure. **11 . . . B-K1 12
P-QR3 Q-Q2 13 P-KN4!** Restricting Black's options on the K-side before
returning his attentions to the Q-side advance. **13 . . . N-B2 14 N-QB3
P-R3 15 P-R4 Q-B1** Paradoxically Black cannot afford to seal the Q-side
with . . . P-QR4 because then White would be able to castle long and
launch an attack against the black king, for which the move 13 P-KN4
would come in very handy. **16 P-R3** Overprotecting the KNP to free the
queen. **16 . . . R-N1 17 Q-B2 B-Q2 18 P-N3 P-N3 19 N-Q1 P-QN4** Now
the game takes on a Benoni-like structure. **20 P-R5 K-R1 21 B-N3 N-N1
22 N-K3 N-K2 23 B-R4** Preventing . . . P-B4. **23 . . . Q-K1 24 P-N4!**
Carefully calculated. If 24 . . . BP×P 25 P-B5, with threats of P-B6 and
P×P. **24 . . . N-B1 25 NP×P QP×P 26 P×P N×NP 27 B×N** Obviously the
knight can not be permitted to reach . . . Q5. **27 . . . R×B 28 0-0!** Now
that Black's Q-side pawn structure has been ruined, White calmly puts his
king into safety cashing in on Black's numerous Q-side weaknesses. **28 . . .
P-B4 29 P-B3 R-B2 30 N(2)-B4 R-N5 31 B-K1 R-N2 32 B-B3 P-R4 33
NP×BP P×P 34 P×P P-K5 35 K-R2 P×P 36 R×P B-Q5 37 Q-Q3 B-KB3
38 R-KN1** Since Black has compromised his position on the K-side,
Petrosian decides to switch his attack. **38 . . . K-R2 39 B×B R×B 40
Q-B3 Q-B1 41 R-N6 R-KB2 42 R-N5** Black Resigned After 42 . . .
Q-R3 43 R-N6 Q-B1 (repeating the position) White would play 44 N-K5,
when Black's game collapses at once. This game was a convincing example
of how White can advance on the Q-side even after Black's . . . P-QB4.

Thematic Ideas for White
In the previous example we saw how the move P-KN4 can help White to
keep his opponent's K-side counterplay under firm control. Such preventive

measures by White can even be played after he has castled K-side, without
too much fear of the idea rebounding.

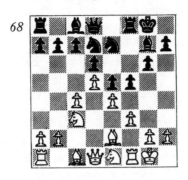

Ribli–Ciocaltea   Moscow 1977

11 P-KN4 The idea behind this move is to stifle Black's K-side attack
before it can make any progress. If Black plays ... P-KB5, White will
advance P-KR4 and then seal up the K-side altogether, meeting ... P-KN4
with P-KR5 and ... P-KR4 with P-N5. Black cannot afford to allow the
K-side to become closed as this would leave him at the mercy of White's
advance on the other wing. It is therefore essential for Black to maintain
the tension in the K-side, hoping that the advance P-KN4 will eventually
prove weakening for White. Black should also try to create some activity in
the centre, since a central counter-blow is often the most successful
strategy against an advance on the wing. For this reason Black does better
to play ... P-QB3 (attacking the centre) than ... P-QB4 (closing the
centre). **11 ... N-KB3 12 N-Q3 P-B4?** Now White has nothing to worry
about and can increase his command of both K-side and Q-side. After
12 ... P-B3! Black would have sufficient counterplay to maintain the
balance. **13 B-Q2 P-KR3 14 P-KR4 P-R3 15 N-B2 B-Q2 16 P-R3 P-QR4
17 P-N3 N-K1 18 K-N2 N-B2 19 B-Q3 P-B5** Now White will have no
further worries on the K-side and can turn his attention to the advance on
the other wing. **20 R-R1 N-B1 21 P-R5 P-KN4** The first part of White's
plan has been executed, depriving Black of any counterplay. **22 P-N4**
Black's forces are rather badly placed to cope with this opening up of the
Q-side, while White's space advantage makes it all the more easy for him to
prosecute his attack. **22 ... RPXP 23 PXP RXR 24 QXR PXP 25 N-R2
N-R3 26 R-QN1 N-N3 27 NXP N-B4 28 Q-R7 N-B1 29 Q-R2 N-N3 30
Q-R7 N-B1 31 Q-R3 N-N3 32 N-R2 N(N3)-R5 33 N-B3 NXN 34 BXN
Q-R1 35 B-N4 P-N3 36 R-QR1 Q-N2 37 B-K2 R-QN1 38 N-Q1 Q-B2
39 N-B3 B-KB1 40 K-B1 R-N2 41 K-K1 R-N1 42 K-Q2 R-N2** Black
is helpless. He can do nothing while White prepares for the endgame. **43
R-R2 R-N1 44 K-B1 R-N2 45 K-Q2 B-K2 46 B-Q1 K-B2 47 BXN** At

last White reveals his plan. He intends to penetrate on the light squares. **47 ... NP×B 48 B–R4 R–N5 49 B×B Q×B 50 Q–R6 B–Q1 51 N–N5 K–K2 52 Q–R8** Black resigns

Golden rules for Classical Positions

1) Black must play for ... P–KB4 and a K-side advance.

2) White must play for P–QB5 and/or P–QN4, with a Q-side attack.

3) Black must not allow the K-side pawns to become locked, otherwise he will be left without any counterplay.

4) Black must be careful when deciding between ... P–QB3 and ... P–QB4. The solid looking ... P–QB4 will not necessarily stifle White's Q-side attack, whereas the double-edged looking ... P–QB3 will sometimes be Black's best road to counterplay.

5) If White exchanges his K4 pawn for Black's ... KB4 pawn, Black should, more often than not, recapture with the KNP.

6 The Petrosian System

The basic position of the Petrosian System arises after the moves **1 P–Q4 N–KB3 2 P–QB4 P–KN3 3 N–QB3 B–N2 4 P–K4 P–Q3 5 N–B3 0–0 6 B–K2 P–K4 7 P–Q5**.

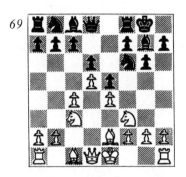

69

For more than twenty years, since its invention, the Petrosian System, which involves a subsequent B–KN5 by White, has been one of the most important lines against the King's Indian.

The original concept of the Petrosian System was purely strategical. White aims to entice the pawn advance ... P–KR3 and ... P–KN4 and thus reduce Black's king's bishop to a chronic state of blockade by its own pawns. If, later on, White can force the exchange of the opposing light-squared bishop, his knights then have a free run of the light squares with close to a strategically won game.

Black's counter-chances against this strategy lie in utilizing the extra time, created by the slowness of White's manoeuvres, for aggressive king-side action. If Black can establish his knight at KB5 and then create a fluid centre by ... P–KB4 and ... P–KN4–5, then his active pieces have good prospects.

More recently an alternative White strategy has evolved. After Black's pawns have been weakened by ... P–KR3 and ... P–KN4, White switches to a direct king-side attack with P-KR4, with the option, according to how Black defends, of a direct assault on the king or a reversion to the underlying light square theme. This method leads to very sharp play, and a final verdict has not yet been reached.

Though overall practical results in the Petrosian System favour White, the fact that grandmasters of the calibre of Gligorić, Geller and, until his premature death, Stein continue to defend it successfully shows that the system is far from a positional refutation of the King's Indian.

Let us now look at what happened in the first game played with the System.

Petrosian–Suetin   U.S.S.R. Championship 1958
**1 P-Q4 N-KB3 2 P-QB4 P-KN3 3 N-QB3 B-N2 4 P-K4 P-Q3 5 B-K2 0-0
6 N-B3 P-K4 7 P-Q5 QN-Q2 8 B-N5**

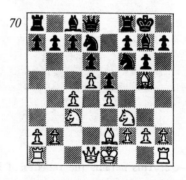

70

The pin does not seem particularly dangerous since White cannot increase his pressure against the knight on KB6. In addition, the black queen can easily remove herself from the pin by side-stepping to any suitable square, such as . . . QR4, . . . K1, . . . QB2 etc. However, the plan behind B-KN5 is a deep one. In order to free himself from the pin, which hampers his counterplay on the king's wing, Black is most likely to play . . . P-KR3 and . . . P-KN4, chasing the white bishop to the rather unusual square KN3. But this pawn advance weakens the squares . . . KB4 and . . . KN5, thus giving White a foothold for neutralizing Black's play on that wing. At the same time White has very good opportunities for a pawn storm on the other wing.

8 . . . P-KR3 9 B-R4 P-KN4 10 B-N3 N-R4 11 0-0 P-QR4 12 N-K1 N-B5 13 N-B2

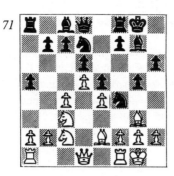

71

White's plans are developing. He ignores the black knight's invasion on KB4 and continues to increase the grip on the KB5 and KN4 squares, simultaneously hemming in the bishop on KN7. **13 ... N-B4** A small but significant error. Correct was 13 ... P-KB4 14 PXP NXB+ (14 ... N-B3 15 B-N4!) 15 QXN N-B3 followed by ... BXP. In that event Black could have fought more or less successfully. Now White gradually takes over the game and his positional aims bear fruit. **14 N-K3 NXKP** Otherwise 15 B-N4. **15 NXN NXB+ 16 QXN P-KB4 17 P-B3 P-B5** 17 ... PXN 18 PXP R-B5 19 BXR KPXB 20 N-B5 is no better for Black. **18 P-B5 PXN** After 18 ... PXB 19 RPXP and P-KN4, White's knights would have been far superior to Black's bishops. **19 QXP B-B4 20 QR-B1 Q-Q2 21 R-B4 PXP** Otherwise White takes on Q6 and then penetrates with his queen to QN6. **22 QXBP P-N3 23 Q-K3 QXP** 23 ... R-B2, covering the ... QB2 square, offered more chances of effective resistance, **24 RXP Q-Q5** 24 ... QXP 25 N-Q6 Q-Q4 26 R-K1! **25 B-B2! QXQ** The exchange of queens does not help. It might have been better to try 25 ... QXP. **26 BXQ B-K3 27 P-QR3 P-N4 28 B-Q2!** This heralds the transfer of bishop to QB3 and rook to K1, with the prospect of the manoeuvre N-N3-R5. **28 ... KR-Q1 29 B-B3 P-R5 30 R-K1 QR-B1 31 R-N7 R-Q4** 31 ... R-N1 32 RXB+ KXR 33 BXP+ wins a pawn. **32 R-N6 B-B2** 32 ... B-Q2 33 RXRP! **33 N-Q6 R-Q1 34 N-B5 K-R2 35 R-N7 R1-Q2 36 RXR RXR 37 NXB KXN 38 RXP K-N3 39 RXQNP** Despite the bishops of opposite colours the ending is now a clear win for White. **39 ... R-Q8+ 40 K-B2 R-QB8 41 R-N6+ K-R2 42 P-KN4 R-KR8 43 P-R3 B-Q4** 43 ... RXP 44 K-N2 R-R5 45 B-K1. **44 R-Q6 R-Q8 45 R-Q7+ K-N1 46 K-K3 B-N6 47 R-KN7+ K-B1 48 R-N6 B-B7 49 RXRP R-Q6+ 50 K-K2 R-Q4 51 P-R4 PXP 52 RXP K-B2 53 P-B4 B-Q8+ 54 K-K3 K-N3 55 P-N5 B-R4 56 B-B6 R-QB4 57 K-Q4 R-N4 58 K-K4 B-Q8 59 P-B5+ K-B2 60 B-K5 B-B7+ 61 K-B4 Black resigns.**

White's Basic Strategy
1) To achieve light-square domination.

2) To induce the self-incarceration of Black's dark-square bishop by its own pawns.

3) To exchange light-squared bishops, thus giving his knights free rein (bear in mind the possibility of a good knight v. bad bishop ending).

4) To carry through the standard King's Indian type queen-side attack.

5) An alternative strategy is to play more directly with an advance of the KRP, looking for a king-side attack.

Black's Basic Strategy

1) To take aggressive king-side action.

2) To establish a knight at . . . KB5.

3) To create chances on the king-side by advancing with . . . P–KB4 and P–KN4–5.

4) To play . . . P–QB4 to hold up White's queen-side advance, perhaps in combination with . . . N–QR3, or

5) To play . . . P–QR4 and place a knight on . . . QB4, with the same aim.

Many of these themes occur in all Petrosian System games, so let us now look at some examples, first of all examining an important question.

The exchange of dark-squared bishops

Should Black try to exchange his dark-squared bishop? If he does try, should White, in turn, try to avoid it? The traditional view is that the exchange is advantageous for Black. However, White's dark-squared bishop can sometimes be quite bad, despite having almost all his pawns on light squares. Another factor to be considered is that after an exchange of dark-squared bishops, Black's king is deprived of an important defender. Probably there can be no definite answer to the above questions, but consider carefully the following example.

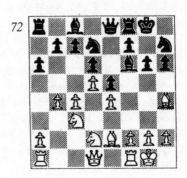

72

Tal–Fischer   Candidates Tournament 1959
13 B×B N/R2×B 14 N–N3 Q–K2 15 Q–Q2 K–R2 16 Q–K3 Black is unable, without considerable positional sacrifices, to prevent the break-through by P–QB5. **16 . . . N–KN1!** By defending his queen, Black assures himself of future counterplay based on his K4 square. **17 P–B5 P–B4 18 KP×P NP×P 19 P–B4 KP×P 20 Q×P P×P 21 B–Q3!** 'White spent his time deciding between the continuation in the game and the variation: 21 P×P N×P 22 QR–B1 B–Q2! 23 Q×QBP QR–B1 24 Q–B4 N×N 25 P×N R×N 26 R×R Q×B 27 R–B7 Q–K2 28 P–Q6 Q–K3, when, despite the active placing of the white pieces, there is apparently no decisive continuation. Now, however, White's threats become considerably more concrete in character.' –Tal. **21 . . . P×P** If Black tries to hold back the attack with 21 . . . Q–N2, then 22 B×BP+ K–R1 23 N–K4 N–K4 24 N–N3 N–K2 25 QR–K1, and if 25 . . . B×B, then 26 Q×N, while on 25 . . . N–Q6, 26 R×N is possible. **22 QR–K1 Q–B3** 'This is the decisive mistake. 22 . . . Q–Q3 was better, when play would probably have continued as follows: 23 B×BP+ K–R1 24 Q–Q4+ Q–B3 25 Q×P Q–QN3+ 26 Q–Q4+ Q×Q+ 27 N×Q with a considerable positional advantage for White. Now events develop by force.'–Tal. **23 R–K6 Q×N 24 B×BP+ R×B 25 Q×R+ K–R1 26 R–B3 Q–N7 27 R–K8 N–B3 28 Q×N+ Q×Q 29 R×Q K–N2 30 R/B6–B8 N–K2 31 N–R5**

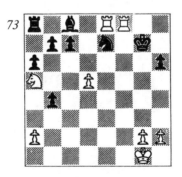

73

'An amusing position: Black's king, knight and bishop have no moves, while he cannot advance his BP since White gets a passed pawn, nor his NP in view of N–B6. On 31 . . . R–R2 White does not have to capture on QB8, but can win a piece simply by moving his rook away from B8.'–Tal. **31 . . . P–R4 32 P–KR4 R–N1 33 N–B4 P–N4 34 N–K5 and Black resigned.**

Black's knight reaches . . . KB5

74

Nei–Stein   U.S.S.R. Championship 1963

If White takes the knight then Black, of course, should recapture with his KP. Then his pieces obtain many new lines: the dark-squared bishop springs to life on the a1-h8 diagonal, the queen and rooks get the K-file and the knight can jump to and from . . . K4. **12 P×P P×P 13 B–B1** Better 13 Q–B2, keeping pieces as active as possible, e.g. 13 . . . N×NP+ 14 K–Q2! P–N5 15 QR–KN1! P×N 16 B×BP N–B5 17 B×N P×B 18 P–K5 with a strong attack for White. **13 . . . P–KB4 14 N–Q2 N–B4 15 Q–B2 P–B3 16 P–B3 QBP×P 17 BP×P P×P 18 N/Q2×P N×N 19 P×N P–R3 20 B–B2 P–N5!** with good counterplay for Black. The game was eventually drawn.

White's P–KR4 leads to a king-side attack

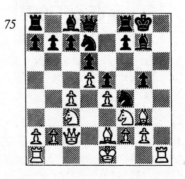

75

Black has got his knight to . . . KB5 and should now consolidate. **13 . . . N×NP+** This move only serves to open another line for White's planned king-side attack; better 13 . . . P–KB4 14 P×P N–B4. **14 K–Q2! Q–B3.** Not the best, but White will, in any case, get a strong attack. **15 QR–KN1 N–B5**

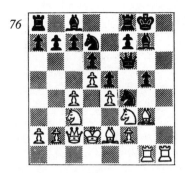

76

16 N×NP!! B-R3 White wins after 16 ... Q×N **17 B-R4 Q-R3 18 B-N5 Q-N3 19 B×N! 17 K-K1 N-KN3** If 17 ... B×N, **18 B-R4! 18 N-K6!! P×N 19 R×B K-B2 20 B-R5 R-KN1 21 B-R4** and Black can no longer hold back White's attack.

Black tries to hold back White's queen-side advance

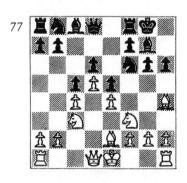

77

Geller-Ljubojević Petropolis 1973

9 ... N-R3 The knight here combines with the QBP to hold up White's queen-side play. It can, in due course, go to ... QB2 to support Black's own queen-side break with ... P-QN4, **10 N-Q2** This is an extremely common move in the Petrosian System — White increases his light-square grip and deters Black from attempting to manoeuvre his knight to ... KB5. **10 ... Q-K1 11 0-0 N-R2** With his queen-side secure, Black prepares P-KB4. White now has a choice between the usual queen-side advance and becoming active on the king-side. **12 N-N5!** This causes some congestion in Black's already restricted position. **12 ... Q-Q2 13 B-N3!** White prepares for P-B4 which, since Black will have little option but to exchange, will add greatly to the pressure against the pawn at Q6. **13 ... N-B2 14 P-B4 P×P 15 B×P N-K1 16 N-B3 Q-K2** Black has defended his QP and is trying to control ... K4, but it is a difficult task. **17 Q-Q2 P-N4 18 B-N3**

N/R2–B3 **19 B–Q3 N–R4** Not 19 . . . N×KP 20 B×N Q×B 21 N×QP N×N 22 B×N R–Q1 23 B–B7 R–Q2 24 P–Q6 with QR–K1 to follow, leaving Black helpless. **20 B–B2 N–B5** Black's knight arrives at . . . KB5, he has held back White's queen-side advance and his dark-squared bishop has an open diagonal. Thus he has achieved many of his objectives, yet White not only has the initiative but can even choose to operate almost anywhere on the board and Black's position is rather constricted. **21 QR–K1 P–R3 22 N–B3 N–N3 23 P–KR3 K–R1?** It really was time to occupy . . . K4 with the knight, or even with the bishop. **24 B–N3 Q–B2 25 P–KR4! P–N5 26 P–R5! P×N 27 P×N P/B2×P**

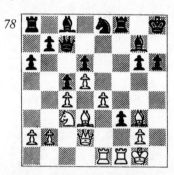

78

28 P–K5! White's pieces now spring to life and Black's king-side with the KRP on R3—remember White's B–KN5?—is indefensible. **28 . . . B–B4 29 R×P P×P 30 B×B R×B 31 R×R P×R 32 B×P! Q–N3** If 32 . . . B×B, then 33 Q×P+ K–N1 34 Q–K6+ and White wins. **33 P–Q6 K–R2** Or 33 . . . B×B 34 R×B N×QP (34 . . . Q×QP 35 R×N+) 35 Q×P+ and 36 R–K7. **34 N–Q5 Q–Q1 35 P–Q7! Q–R5 36 Q–KB2 Q×Q+ 37 K×Q B×B 38 R×B N–Q3 39 R–K8 R×R 40 N–B6+ and Black resigned.**

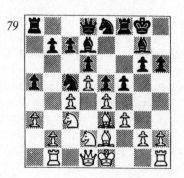

79

Calvo–A. Rodriguez   Buenos Aires (Olympiad) 1978
Black has elected to adopt one of the set-ups for restraining White's queen-side play. In addition, he has succeeded in preparing and playing . . .

P–KB4. **14 P–QN4** White continues according to plan. **14 ... RPXP 15
RPXP N–R5 16 Q–B2 N–B3 17 0–0 NXN 18 QXN P–B5 19 B–B2 P–KN4
20 R–R1 R–N1 21 P–B5** The first achievement of White's queen-side play
and **21 ... P–N5** of Black's king-side advance. **22 KR–B1**

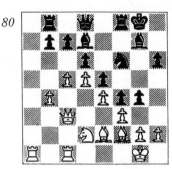

80

22 ... P–N6! **23 RPXP BPXP 24 BXP N–R4 25 B–B2 Q–N4** Black's
pawn sacrifice has gained him time to bring some of his pieces into action
on the king-side. **26 K–B1 N–B5** Occupying the good square with the
usual, and correct, piece. **27 P–N3 Q–R4!** **28 K–K1** The only move. If
28 PXN?, 28 ... Q–R8+ 29 B–N1 B–R6+ 30 K–B2 KPXP wins. **28 ...
Q–R8+ 29 B–B1 N–R6!** **30 Q–K3 N–N4 31 R–R3 B–N4 32 K–Q1 NXBP**
What of White's theme of light-square domination? It has been turned
completely upside down. **33 NXN QXB+ 34 K–Q2 Q–R6 35 PXP PXP
36 Q–N6 B–B8!** **37 N–R4 B–B3 38 R/B1–B3 B–KN4+ 39 K–B2 B–N7 40
N–B3 Q–N5!** **41 QXQP QXKP+ 42 K–N2 BXN 43 RXB Q–K7+ 44 K–N1
Q–Q8+ 45 K–R2 Q–B7+ 46 K–R1 RXR!** **47 QXR+** Of course, if 47 RXR,
then 47 ... R–R1+ wins. **47 ... R–B1 and White resigned.**

7 Fianchetto Variations with . . . P–K4

One of White's most popular continuations against the King's Indian Defence is the kingside fianchetto (P-KN3 and B-N2). Against this rather non-committal system by White, Black has a number of satisfactory defences. He can strike back in the centre by . . . P-K4 or . . . P-QB4 or he can omit both these moves and seek counterplay elsewhere. The present chapter is devoted to systems in which Black plays . . . P-K4. Other systems for Black will be considered in the following chapter.

A typical position in the P-KN3 . . . P-K4 system arises after the following moves:- **1 P-Q4 N-KB3 2 P-QB4 P-KN3 3 N-KB3 B-N2 4 P-KN3 0-0 5 B-N2 P-Q3 6 0-0 QN-Q2 7 N-B3 P-K4 8 P-K4 P-B3 9 P-KR3**

81
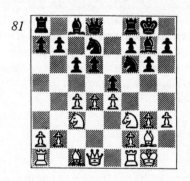

Strategic Features of Diagram
1) Both kings are safe. Compared to other variations of the King's Indian Defence White's fianchettoed KB makes it more difficult for Black to launch a successful attack on White's king. In practice, games in this variation are rarely decided by direct kingside attacks. The theatres of war are usually the centre and queen-side. King's fianchetto systems are therefore not suitable for White players who like to attack the king at all costs.

2) White has a space advantage. This means he has more room in which to manoeuvre his pieces than Black. Black should therefore try to bring the game to the boil early, before White has time to out-manoeuvre him.

3) Black's position, although a little cramped, is very solid. His only potential weakness is his pawn on . . . Q3. In contrast White has played ambitiously in the centre and his pawns on QB4, Q4 and K4 could all become targets. Black should try to attack these targets before White has time to consolidate.

4) White has the option of radically altering the strategic nature of the position by playing P-Q5. Whether he does so is partly a matter of taste —some people prefer blocked positions, others open positions. Positions with a blocked centre are so different from positions with an open centre that they will be considered separately at the end of this chapter.

White's Basic Strategy

To exploit his space advantage to crush Black which means:-

1) Massing his pieces in the centre ready for offensive or defensive purposes.

2) Being constantly aware of Black's tactical possibilities so as to be able either (a) to nip Black's tactics in the bud or (b) to invite Black to overreach himself.

3) Ultimately, when White has consolidated his position and Black is left without counterplay, to select a suitable target for attack. What this target should be depends very much on what Black has been up to. Often the target will be Black's pawn on Q6.

4) If things go wrong and White cannot prevent all Black's tactical threats White should try to cut his losses. It is usually possible to give Black quite a few problems even after he has won a pawn. But in practice White often becomes demoralised and allows Black to win more material than necessary. Do not fall into this trap!

Black's Basic Strategy

To play actively in order to knock White off his balance before White has a chance to consolidate which means:-

1) Selecting one or more targets. White's QB and K pawns are the most common targets. White's QN, Q, KB, and KR pawns may also serve as targets and on occasion Black can even try attacking White's pieces e.g. a knight on QB3 or Q4.

2) Attacking the target rapidly so that White has to disrupt the harmony of his position in order to defend it.

3) Ultimately being on the lookout for the rapid switch to a different target.

4) If things go wrong and you really must fall back on the defensive keep

alive to possibilities of leaping out again. Black's position is very resilient. It is difficult for White to tie him down permanently.

Ideal Wins for White and Black

Our outline of the basic stratey for White and Black shows the importance of the ·time factor. The early middlegame usually develops into a race in which White tends to consolidate before Black has time to do anything dangerous and Black tends to prevent White from consolidating. We will now consider two concrete examples of such a race, the first won by Black and the second by White. These games illustrate ideal wins by Black and White in this variation.

Ideal Win for Black

Zita-Bronstein   Prague-Moscow 1941

1 P–QB4 P–K4 2 N–QB3 N–KB3 3 N–KB3 P–Q3 4 P–Q4 QN–Q2 5 P–KN3 P–KN3 6 B–N2 B–N2. We have now reached a King's Indian position more often arrived at via the move order 1 P–Q4 N–KB3 2 P–QB4 P–KN3 3 N–KB3 B–N2 4 P–KN3 P–Q3 5 B–N2 QN–Q2 6 N–QB3 P–K4. Such transpositional possibilities are common in the King's Indian. **7 0–0 0–0 8 P–QN3** White plans to fianchetto his queen's bishop. This idea is just playable but it requires very careful handling by White. The queen's bishop is usually better placed on K3 in this variation. **8 . . . P–B3?** 8 . . . R–K1 is more accurate since 9 B–R3! attacking Black's weak Q-pawn would now have been good for White. If Black then played 9 . . . Q–B2 10 PXP would be strong since 10 . . . PXP would allow 11 BXR. Note that after 9. . . R–K1 9 B–N2 P–B3 10 B–QR3 is no longer good for White as Black can play 10 . . . Q–B2 and if 11 PXP PXP 12 B–Q6 Q–R4 White's bishop is misplaced on Q6. **9 B–N2? R–K1 10 P–K4 PXP 11 NXP Q–N3** Already we have seen one disadvantage of White's queenside fianchetto. If White's bishop were on K3 it would discourage Black from developing his queen on this good square. **12 Q–Q2?** The queen belongs on QB2 where it can keep an eye on the potentially weak pawns on N3 and K4. The immediate 12 Q–B2 was impossible in view of 12 . . . QXN and so White should have played 12 R–K1 or 12 P–KR3 intending to play Q–B2 in reply to . . . N–B4. **12 . . . N–B4** Attacking White's K pawn. **13 KR–K1 P–QR4!** Now Black selects White's N pawn as a target. **14 QR–N1 P–R5 15 B–QR1** If White captured on R4 his QR and QB pawns would become very weak. **15 . . . PXP 16 PXP N–N5!** If White had had time to play P–R3 to prevent this move his position would not be too bad. Now Black's pieces come flooding into his position. **17 P–R3!** Too late! Comparatively best was 17 P–N4 even though it weakens White's QB pawn.

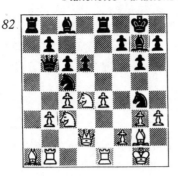

82

17 . . . R×B! This undermines the protection of N3 and preposes Black's next blow. **18 R×R N×KBP!** Now both 19 K×N N×NP and 19 Q×N N–Q6 are disastrous for White. Note how Black exploits the weakness of Black's knight on . . . Q5. **19 R–K3** White has nothing better in view of the threat of 19 N(either)–Q6. Now the game turns into a rout. The remaining moves were **19 . . . N×P+ 20 K–R2 N–B7 21 R–B3 N/B4×KP 22 Q–B4 N–N5+ 23 K–R1 P–KB4 24 N×N R×N 25 Q×QP R×N 26 Q–N8 R–Q1 27 R–R8 B–K4 28 Q–R7 Q–N5 29 Q–N1 Q–B1 30 B–R3 Q–R3.** White resigned.

Ideal Win for White

In the previous game Black won the race to disrupt White's position before White had time to consolidate. In the following game Black does not seem aware that such a race is in existence. White is allowed to build up a dominating position undisturbed. Black never gets any counterplay and is mercilessly crushed.

Whiteley–Lambshire English Club Championship 1967
1 P–Q4 N–KB3 2 P–QB4 P–KN3 3 N–KB3 B–N2 4 P–KN3 0–0 5 B–N2 P–Q3 6 0–0 QN–Q2 7 N–B3 P–K4 8 P–K4 P–QB3 9 P–KR3 R–K1 10 B–K3 P–KR3? This move is a waste of time. Black may have wished to prevent B–N5 but there was no need. Black can always play P–KR3 after B–N5 when White is faced with the unpleasant alternatives of B–R4? allowing the bishop to be trapped by . . . P–KN4, B×N surrendering the two bishops and the retreat B–K3 which admits that B–N5 was a waste of time. Better moves for Black were 10 . . . P–QR4 or 10 . . . P×P. **11 Q–B2 P–QR4 12 QR–Q1 Q–B2 13 KR–K1 K–R2.** More time wasting.

83
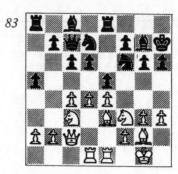

White now has a space advantage and a lead in development. He now needs to break open the position in order to exploit these advantages. **14 P–B5!** This pawn sacrifice, a common resource against passive play by Black, suits White's purpose admirably. **14 . . . QP×P.** White threatened 15 BP×P and if 15 . . . Q×P 16 P×P winning a piece. If 14 . . . KP×P 15 P×P Q×P 16 N×P threatening among other things 17 P–B4 and 18 P–K5 is very strong for White. **15 P×KP N×KP(4)** If 15 . . . N–R4 16 P–KN4 wins a piece. **16 N×N Q×N 17 P–B4 Q–K2 18 P–K5 N–Q2 19 N–K4 P–B3 20 N–Q6 R–Q1?** 20 . . . R–B1 would have prevented White's following combination but Black would still have had a hopelessly passive position. **21 Q×P+! K×Q 22 B–K4+ K–R4 23 P–N4+ K–R5 24 K–N2** Black resigned as he cannot prevent 25 B–B2 mate.

It is unusual for White to be able to deliver checkmate so early in this opening. But in the present game Black allowed White such a free hand in the centre that it was easy for White to convert this central advantage into a decisive kingside attack.

Having seen what can happen if White or Black goes horribly wrong, we now consider various recurrent themes in this opening.

White Omits P–K4

After the moves **1 P–Q4 N–KB3 2 P–QB4 P–KN3 3 N–KB3 B–N2 4 P–KN3 0–0 5 B–N2 P–Q3 6 0–0 QN–Q2 7 N–B3 P–K4** we reach Diagram 84

84

White's normal move in this position is 8 P-K4. What happens if White omits this move? **8 P-N3 R-K1 9 B-N2 P-B3**. The immediate 9 . . . P-K5 is not so good, in view of the variation 10 N-N5 P-K6 11 BPXP and if 11 . . . N-N5? 12 NXBP Q-K2 13 N-Q5! **10 Q-B2?** White should play 10 P-K3 in order to prevent Black's following manoeuvre. But this unambitious pawn advance would leave Black with a comfortable game. **10 . . . P-K5! 11 N-KN5** 11 N-Q2 is worse since after 11 . . . P-K6 the knight is attacked and so White has no time for 12 P-B4. **11 . . . P-K6! 12 BPXP!** Comparatively best is 12 P-B4 but Black's pawn on K3 is then an uncomfortable thorn in White's flesh. **13 . . . N-N5.**

85

Black now stands very well. He threatens both 14 . . . QXN and 14 . . . NXP(K6). If White plays 14 NXBP the continuation could be 14 . . . Q-K2 renewing the threat on K3. 15 Q-Q3 NXP(K6) 16 R-B3 N-KB4 and Black threatens 17 . . . BXP+ and 17 . . . QXN.

Conclusion
. . . P-K5 and . . . P-K6 is the stock antidote when White omits P-K4. Black should time this advance carefully to ensure that White cannot advantageously play N-KN5 and NXBP.

White Plays QPXP
In Diagram 84 above White often plays 8 PXP. This move is not, however, to be recommended unless White is satisfied with a draw and so wishes to avoid the more complex positions arising after 8 P-K4. 8 PXP releases the tension in the centre and so allows Black easy equality.

Here is an example of how Black can obtain the advantage after indifferent play by White.

8 PXP PXP 9 P-K4? This move is best avoided after the exchange of pawns on K5, since it creates a slight weakness on White's Q4. 9 . . . P-B3! This ensures that . . . Q4 does not become a corresponding weakness in Black's position. 10 Q-Q6? A tempting move but White's queen in fact achieves nothing here. 10 . . . Q-N3 11 P-N3 R-K1 12 B-N5 P-QR4 13

BXN BXB 14 QR–Q1 B–K2 15 Q–Q2 B–N5 After the exchange of pawns on K5 Black's bishop has little scope on N2 and it is often useful to redeploy it on the queenside. It is not so easy for White to redeploy his inactive bishop on N2. 16 Q–B2 N–B1 Since the position is rather blocked Black has time for a long winded manoeuvure to strengthen his control of Q4. Other routes by which Black sometimes manoeuvres a knight to Q5 in this variation are . . . N–KB3–Q2–QB4–K3–Q5 and . . . N–KB3–Q2–B1– K3–Q5. 17 R–Q2 B–N5 18 P–KR3 BXKN 19 BXB N–K3.

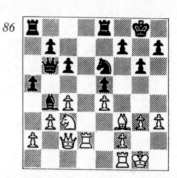

86

Black has a distinct positional advantage in view of his control of the black squares and in particular Q4.

Conclusion
QPXP is not dangerous for Black. If White follows this exchange up with P–K4 (or plays it when he already has a pawn on K4) Black should concentrate on exploiting White's weak square Q4.

Black Omits . . . P–B3
Returning to Diagram 84 play normally continues 8 P–K4 P–B3; . . . P–B3 is not an essential move for Black and Black sometimes omits it in order to avoid weakening his . . . Q3 pawn. The disadvantage is that without . . . P–B3 Black is unable to develop his queen on the active squares . . . N3 or . . . R4 and White may be able to post a knight on QN5 or Q5. From Diagram 84 play could continue 8 P–K4 PXP 9 NXP R–K1 10 R–K1 N–B4 11 P–KR3 P–QR4 12 N(Q4)–N5. With this move White tries to punish Black for omitting . . . P–QB3. The move . . . P–QB3 is now permanently ruled out in view of the reply NXQP. It may in fact be better for White to play 12 Q–B2. The tempting 12 . . . N(B3)XKP then fails to 13 NXN BXN 14 B–N5 Q–Q2. (Not 14 . . . P–KB3 15 BXP! BXB 16 NXB+ QXN 17 RXR+ and wins.) 15 N–B6+ BXN 16 BXB and the weakness of the dark squares around Black's king gives White more than enough compensation for his sacrificed pawn. After 12 Q–B2 Black may have nothing better than

to play 12 . . . P–B3 after all. White then obtains a slight plus by 13 B–B4 aiming at the weak Q6 pawn. Note that where Black plays an early . . . P–B3 White has normally developed his bishop on K3 before Black plays . . . P×P and so White does not have the opportunity to play B–B4 in one move. **12 . . . B–Q2** This falls in with White's plans. Black should play more actively by 12 . . . KN–Q2 13 B–K3 N–K4 and if 14 B×N (14 P–N3 may be better) 14 . . . P×B 15 Q×Q R×Q 16 N×P R–N1 and Black has good compensation for the pawn. **13 B–B4 B–B3 14 Q–B2 KN–Q2 15 QR–Q1 N–K3 16 B–K3.**

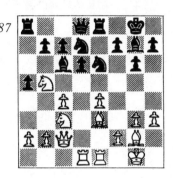

87

Black has a cramped position.

Conclusion
It is safest for Black to play an early . . . P–B3. He may be able to get away with omitting this move but he runs the risk either of obtaining a cramped position or being forced to play . . . P–B3 later in less favourable circumstances.

White Omits P–KR3
P–KR3 is a useful move for White. It prevents Black's queen's bishop reaching . . . N5 and often makes it hard for Black to find a suitable square on which to develop that bishop. It also prevents . . . N–N5 which can be especially dangerous if White has already played B–K3.

Botvinnik–Smyslov   World Championship 1954
From Diagram 84 play continued **8 P–K4 P–QB3 9 B–K3** (9P–KR3!) **9 . . . N–N5 10 B–N5 Q–N3!** Black takes advantage of the misplacement of White's queen's bishop to attack two weak points in White's position— N2 and Q4. **11 P–KR3 P×P** A promising sacrifice. The play now becomes very complicated. **12 N–QR4 Q–R3 13 P×N P–QN4** trapping the knight **14 N×P.** 14 B–K7 may be an improvement. **14 . . . P×N 15 N×P Q×N 16 P–K5 Q×P 17 B×R N×P.**

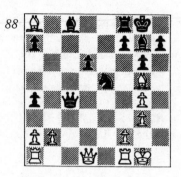

Black has a pawn and a strong attack for the sacrificed exchange. This proved sufficient for a win after further hair-raising complications.

Conclusion
Unless White is willing to enter the maelstrom of complications which occurred in the above game it is safer to play P–KR3.

Black attacks Q4

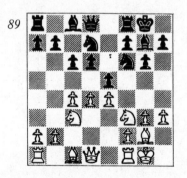

Botvinnik–Geller   Belgrade 1969
From Diagram 89 play continued **9 . . . Q–N3**. Threatening to win a pawn by 10 . . . PXP 11 NXP NXP! **10 R–K1** Defending the pawn since 10 . . . PXP 11 NXP NXP now loses to 12 RXN. The alternative 10 P–Q5 leads to closed positions considered later in this chapter. **10 . . . R–K1 11 R–K2**. A multi-purpose move defending N2 and KB2 and envisaging a later R–B2 or R–Q2 if necessary. Again 11 P–Q5 was a satisfactory alternative. **11 . . . PXP!** Having defended his position by 12 B–K3 after which Black's queen would be misplaced on . . . N3. But Black does not allow White time for this. **12 NXP**

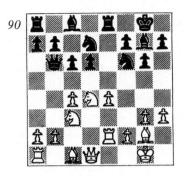

90

12 . . . N–N5! Black exploits White's weakness on Q4 in order to transfer his knight to a more aggressive post on K5. Much weaker were either (a) 12 . . . Q–N5 13 R–B2! indirectly defending the QB pawn since 13 . . . Q×BP loses to 14 N–Q5 and 15 N–B7 or (b) 12 . . . N×KP 13 N×N B×N (If 13 . . . Q×N 14 N–B6+!) 14 N×P R×R 15 Q×R and White stands better. **13 N–B2?** 13 P×N B×N followed by . . . N–K4 was also good for Black. Correct was 13 R–Q2 KN–K4 14 P–N3 leading to a tense position with equal chances. **13 . . . KN–K4 14 N–K3 N–B4 15 P–N3?** A blunder but White's position was already difficult. **15 . . . B×P!** If now 17 B×B N–B6+ 18 K–N2 B×N. So Black won a vital pawn and soon went on to win the game.

Black Attacks White's QB Pawn

Szymczak–Harai   Lublin 1975

From Diagram 89 play coninued **9 . . . Q–N3 10 R–K1 P–QR4** Also good is 10 . . . R–K1 played in the previous extract. **11 R–N1?** Correct was 11 P–Q5 or 11 R–K2. **11 . . . P×P!** Again giving White no time for the consolidating 12 B–K3. **12 N×P N–N5 13 QN–K2** If 13 Q×N or 13 P×N then 13 . . . B×N followed by . . . N–K4 is good for Black. The knight on Q4 cannot move since this would expose White's KB pawn. **13 . . . KN–K4!**

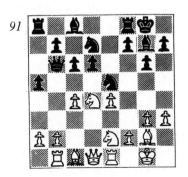

91

Rather surprisingly White now has no satisfactory way to defend the QB pawn. If 14 Q–B2 Q–N5! renews the attack on the pawn and threatens White's rook. **14 P–N3 N×P!** White's N pawn is pinned and so he now loses the QB pawn. Black duly converted this material advantage into a win in 39 moves.

Black's Queen in Difficulty

We have seen how Black's queen can wreak havoc on the queenside if White is not careful. But the early development of Black's queen involves some risk as the following example shows.

Smejkal–Geller   Siegen 1970

From Diagram 89 play continued **9 . . . Q–R4 10 B–K3 Q–N5?** (Correct is 9 . . . P×P 10 N×P N–N3) **11 Q–K2 P×P 12 P–QR3!** (Much stronger than 12 N×P N–N3! when White cannot defend his QB pawn.) **12 . . . Q–R4 13 N×P N–N3 14 KR–Q1 R–K1**

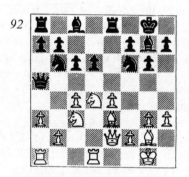

92

15 N/Q4–N5!! If Black captures White's advanced knight his queen is trapped—15 . . . P×N 16 P–QN4! Q–R3 17 P×P. Black tried **15 . . . N×BP** but after 16 Q×N B–K3 17 Q–K2 P×N 18 N×P the weakness of Black's Q pawn proved decisive.

Black Attacks White's K Pawn

Hollis–Gligorić   Hastings 1962/63

From Diagram 89 play continued **9 . . . Q–R4 10 Q–B2 P×P** 10 . . . P–QN4 is stronger. **11 N×P Q–QB4** Black first attacks White's B pawn in order to deflect White's knight from QB3. He then turns his attention to White's K pawn. This is an ambitious plan which turns out better than it should have done. **12 N/B3–K2 R–K1 13 B–K3 Q–K4 14 N–QB3 N–B4**

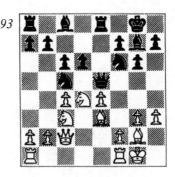

93

White should now have played 15 QR-Q1! with some advantage since it is not safe for Black to take the K pawn, e.g. 15 ... N/B4×P 16 B-B4! and White wins material after either 16 ... Q-K2 17 KR-K1 or 16 ... Q-QB5 17 B×N. Instead White played **15 P-B4 Q-K2 16 B-B2** and Black's strategy was vindicated after **16 ... N/B3×KP 17 N×N N×N 18 B×N B×N!**

Black is Squeezed

Cvetković-Minić   Yugoslavia 1968

From Diagram 89 play continued **9 ... Q-R4 10 B-K3 P×P 11 N×P N-N3 12 N-N3 Q-R3?** (The Queen becomes a target on ... R3. Correct was 12 ... Q-R4.) **13 P-B5 N-B5 14 B-Q4 P×P 15 N×P Q-R4 16 Q-K2 N-K4 17 N-N3 Q-B2 18 P-B4 N/K4-Q2 19 P-K5 N-K1 20 N-K4.**

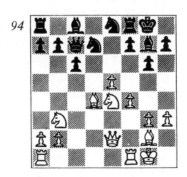

94

White has a huge space advantage and won in only eight more moves.

White Plays P-Q5 and Black Replies ... P-B4

So far we have been considering positions in which the centre remains open. However White can drastically alter the strategic features of the position by closing the centre by P-Q5. The rest of this chapter is devoted to such closed positions.

From Diagram 89 play can continue **9 ... Q-N3 10 P-Q5** This move is also possible against most of Black's other common ninth moves, 9 . . . Q–R4, 9 . . . P–QR4 and 9 . . . R–K1. It is not of course possible if Black plays 9 . . . P×P and so if White is determined to close the centre he should play P–Q5 on move seven or eight. **10 . . . P–B4** The alternative . . . P×P is considered later in this chapter.

95

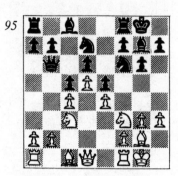

We have now reached the sort of position which arises in the Old Benoni after, e.g. 1 P–Q4 N–KB3 2 P–QB4 P–QB4 3 P–Q5 P–K4 4 N–QB3 P–Q3 5 P–K4 P–KN3 6 N–KB3 B–N2 7 P–KN3 0–0 8 B–N2. Black has lost a tempo by playing . . . P–B4 in two moves but as the position is closed this tempo loss is not very significant.

Most of the principles we have so far explained in this chapter cease to apply once White plays P–Q5. There are no immediate tactical prospects for either side. Therefore, both players will seek a slow build up and there will often be a long period of manoeuvring before the real battle is joined. White will play for a break by P–QR3 and P–QN4 or by P–KB4 and Black will counter either by . . . P–QR3 and . . . P–QN4 or (more often) by . . . P–KB4.

We give two examples of the sort of manoeuvring which can occur.

Keene–Whiteley   England 1968
From Diagram 89 play continued **9 . . . Q–N3 10 R–K1 R–K1 11 P–Q5** This move has added point when Black has played . . . R–K1 since the rook is misplaced on K1 once the centre has been closed. **11 . . . P–B4 12 P–QR3 R–B1 13 R–N1 Q–Q1** Black regroups his forces to prepare for . . . P–B4; **14 P–QN4 P–N3 15 N–QR4 N–K1 16 B–N5!** White has established the advantage on the queenside and if Black remains passive White will double rooks on the N file and eventually play NP×P. Black would then have the unpleasant choice between playing . . . NP×P allowing White play on the open N file and . . . QP×P giving White a protected passed pawn on Q5 and the possibility of undermining Black's queenside by P–QR4–R5. Forced with this long term strategic threat Black's only

chance of counterplay is to play ... P–KB4. White's sixteenth move is an attempt to nip such counterplay in the bud. **16 ... P–B3 17 B–Q2 P–KR3?** If 17 ... P–B4 18 N–N5 eyeing K6 is dangerous for Black. In trying to avoid this, Black falls for something much worse. Correct was 17 ... R–B2 intending ... N–B1 (defending ... N3) and only then ... P–KR3 and ... P–B4. **18 N–R4! P–KN4** (18 ... K–R2 19 Q–N4 is even worse) **19 N–B5**.

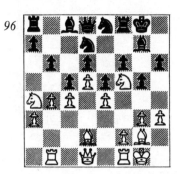

96

Black now has no counterplay. Given the happy choice of breaking through on either wing White chose the kingside and soon built up irresistible pressure.

Sherwin–Fischer   U.S. Championship 1966/7
From Diagram 89 play continued **9 ... Q–N3 10 R–K1 R–K1 11 P–Q5 P–B4 12 P–QR3**, so far as in the previous example. **12 ... P–QR3 13 R–N1 Q–B2 14 B–K3 P–N3 15 B–KB1 N–B1 16 P–QN4 B–Q2 17 K–R2 R/K–N1 18 Q–B2 N–K1 19 R–N2 P–B4**

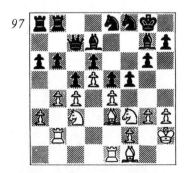

97

Black has taken some precautionary measures on the queenside before playing this thematic move. The position is now about level. There followed further manoeuvring typical of such blocked positions, and Fischer finally outmanoeuvred his opponent to win in 100 moves.

White Plays P–Q5 and Black Replies . . . P×P

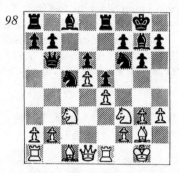

98

The position in the Diagram arises if after P–Q5 Black plays . . . P×P instead of . . . P–B4 and White recaptures BP×P. The position shares many of the strategic features of Diagram 95 but the open QB-file makes an important difference. The centre of gravity of the position is tilted towards the queenside. If Black plays for . . . P–KB4 he is likely to be overwhelmed on the queenside before he can achieve anything on the kingside. Both players therefore usually concentrate on the queenside where White's space advantage gives him slightly the better game. . . . P×P is therefore considered as inferior to . . . P–B4 though it is playable if Black is careful. The following example shows what can happen if Black plays inaccurately.

Keene–Penrose   England 1970
From Diagram 98 play continued **12 . . . B–Q2 13 R–N1 P–QR4 14 B–B1**
Once the centre is blocked the bishop has little future on N2. On KB1 it eyes Black's weak square N5. **14 R/K1–QB1 15 B–K3 Q–Q1 16 N–Q2 N–K1 17 P–QR4 P–B4 18 N–B4 P×P?** (This allows White a strongpoint at K4) **19 B×N R×B 20 N/B3×P R–B2 21 N–N6 R–N1 22 N×B R×N 23 B–N5 R–K2 24 B×N R×B 25 P–QN4 P×P 26 R×P**

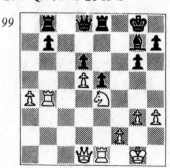

99

White has a classic good knight against bad bishop position. White won in 43 moves.

8 Fianchetto Variations without ... P–K4

In this chapter we consider lines in which White fianchettoes his king's bishop and Black does not reply ... P–K4.

Black's most common alternative central break is ... P–QB4 and after White's normal reply P–Q4 we have the pawn structure shown in Diagrams 100 and 101.

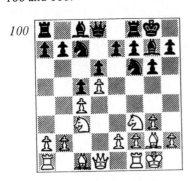 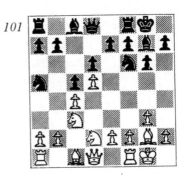

The pawn structure shown in Diagrams 100 and 101, can be reached by many more orders. The most common of these are:

DIAGRAM 100

A 1 P–Q4 N–KB3 2 P–QB4 P–KN3 3 N–KB3 B–N2 4 P–KN3 0–0 5 B–PN2 P–Q3 6 0–0 P–QB4 7 P–Q5 N–QR3 8 N–QB3 N–QB2
B 1 P–Q4 N–KB3 2 P–QB4 P–B4 3 P–Q5 P–Q3 4 N–QB3 P–KN3 5 N–KB3 B–N2 6 P–KN3 0–0 7 B–KN2 N–QR3 8 0–0 N–QB2

DIAGRAM 101

C 1 P–Q4 N–KB3 2 P–QB4 P–KN3 3 N–KB3 B–N2 4 P–KN3 0–0 5 B–N2 P–Q3 6 0–0 P–QB4 7 N–QB3 N–QB3 8 P–Q5 N–QR4 9 N–Q2
D 1 P–Q4 N–KB3 2 P–QB4 P–KN3 3 N–KB3 B–N2 4 P–KN3 0–0 5 B–N2 P–Q3 6 0–0 N–QB3 7 P–Q5 N–QR4 8 KN–Q2 P–QB4 9 N–QB3

Strategic Features of Diagram 100 and 101

1. White has a space advantage since his pawn on Q5 exerts a slight cramping effect on Black's position.

2. Black's bishop on KN2 has more prospects than White's on KN2. The only significant difference between Diagrams 100 and 101 is that in Diagram 100 Black's queen's knight is on QB2 while in Diagram 101 it is on QR4. We shall therefore consider the two positions together.

3. Neither side has any immediate prospects of an attack on the kingside.

4. White's main prospects lie in the centre.

5. Black's main prospects lie on the queenside. He may also be able to challenge White's supremacy in the centre by . . . P-K3 or . . . P-K4.

Ideas for White

1. To play P-K4 and P-K5 in order to cramp Black further in the centre.

2. If Black plays . . . P-K3 or . . . P-K4 to play PXKP and then attack Black's weak pawn on Q3.

3. If Black plays . . . P-K3 to refrain from PXKP and after Black plays . . . PXQP to recapture BPXP transposing into the Modern Benoni Defence.

4. If Black plays . . . P-K4 to refrain from PXP ep and to play for a break on the kingside by P-KB4.

5. To restrain Black's play on the queenside by such precautionary moves as P-QR4, P-QN3, B-N2 and R-N1.

Ideas for Black

1. To play for . . . P-QN4 in order to open the QN-file and attack White's QN2 pawn.

2. If White tries to restrain . . . P-QN4 by P-QR4 Black has a choice between two plans:

(a) Black plays an immediate . . . P-QR3 and after P-QR5 continues . . . P-QN4, PXP ep, RXNP.

(b) Black plays . . . P-QN3 intending to answer P-R5? by . . . P-QN4 when White's pawn becomes weak. Assuming White does not play P-R5 Black plays . . . P-QR3 followed by . . . P-QN4.

Plan b) takes longer but is usually to be preferred since Black is not left with a weak pawn.

3. To strike back in the centre by . . . P-K3 or . . . P-K4. In either case Black must be careful his QP pawn does not become too weak if White opens the centre by PXP(ep).

We will now examine these ideas in further detail.

White Plays P–K5

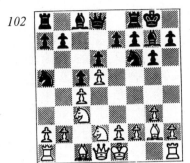

102

Botvinnik–Geller U.S.S.R. Championship 1952

From Diagram 102 play proceeded **9 Q–B2**, usually the best square for the queen in this variation. The queen covers the important squares N2, B3 and B4. **9 . . . P–QR3 10 0–0 B–B4?** Black wastes a move provoking P–K4 which White wants to play anyway. This was an early game in this variation played at a time when it was not generally understood that White's correct strategy is to play for P–K5. **11 P–K4! B–Q2 12 P–N3 P–QN4 13 B–N2 P×P 14 P×P R–N1 15 QR–N1 R–N5 16 P–QR3 R–N1** White has been playing to neutralise Black's operations on the queenside before he attacks in the centre. Black should not have allowed himself to be put off so easily. Correct was 16 . . . R×P with some compensation for the exchange. **17 N–Q1** A standard manoeuvre. The knight heads for K3 where it is well placed for offensive and defensive purposes. **17 . . . Q–B2 18 N–K3 R–N2 19 B–QB3 KR–N1 20 P–R3 R×R 21 R×R R×R+ 22 N×R Q–N3 23 N–Q2 N–K1** This allows the exchange of Black's good bishop. **24 B×B N×B 25 K–R2 N–K1 26 P–B4 N–KB3?** Again Black provokes a move White wishes to play.

103

27 P–K5! The culmination of White's strategy. He now has a massive advantage in the centre and Black has no counterplay on the queenside. **27 . . . N–K1 28 Q–B3 P–B3 29 P–K6** and White soon won.

Black Plays . . . P-QN4

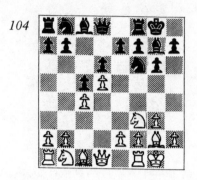

104

Szabo-Gligorić   Leipzig Olympiad 1960
From Diagram 104 play continued **7 . . . N-R3**. When White plays P-Q5
before Black has developed his queen's knight Black no longer has the
option of playing . . . N-B3 and . . . N-R4. Instead he has the choice of
playing . . . N-Q2 or . . . N-R3 and . . . N-B2. Experience has shown that
the knight is much better placed on QB2. On that square it supports
. . . P-QN4 and is well placed if Black plays . . . P-K3. On Q7 it blocks
Black's queen's bishop and makes it difficult for Black to play . . . P-K3
(or . . . P-K4) since after PXP Black's pawn on Q3 is not protected by his
queen. **8 N-QB3 N-QB2 9 B-B4?** Correct was 9 P-QR4. P-QR4 is nearly
always correct when Black's knight is on QB2. However it is usually
better to avoid P-QR4 when Black's knight is on R4 since White's N3
could become weak. **9 . . . P-QN4!** After White's mistake Black is allowed
the luxury of playing this thematic advance without the need for the
preparatory . . . P-QR3. **10 PXP R-N1 11 Q-Q2.** If 11 P-QR4 P-QR3!
12 PXP Black should not be too greedy and play 11 . . . RXP in view of
12 P-R7 R-N2 13 N-QN5! Instead 11 . . . BXP followed by 12 . . . RXP
or 12 . . . R-N5 gives Black a fine game. **11 . . . NXNP 12 B-R6 NXN 13
PXN Q-R4** Not 13 . . . BXB 14 QXB NXP 15 N-N5 N-B3 16 P-K4 with
the powerful threat of P-KB4 and P-K5. **14 BXB KXB** Black already
stands a little better. **15 N-R4 Q-R6 16 P-K4 R-N7 17 Q-B1 B-R3 18
R-K1 KR-N1 19 P-K5 PXP 20 P-Q6? P-K3!** Not 20 . . . PXP 21 N-B5+
PXN 22 Q-N5+ **21 RXP B-Q6 22 R-K1 P-B5.**
    Black soon won White's weakling QR pawn and with it the game.

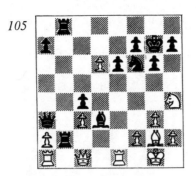

The previous two games were played when the theory of this variation was in its infancy and in each game one of the players went badly wrong. We now give an example of a more modern evenly balanced game.

Whiteley–Kaplan   Hastings 1976/77
From Diagram 104 play continued **7 . . . N–R3 8 N–B3 N–B2 9 P–QR4.**
Improving on 9 B–B4 played in the previous example. **9 . . . R–N1 10 B–B4** This temporarily rules out both . . . P–K3 and . . . P–K4 since Black would lose his Q pawn after P×P. **10 . . . P–N3** 10 . . . P–QR3 11 P–R5 P–QN4 12 P×P ep R×P is also quite playable but Black must then keep a watchful eye on his weak QR pawn. **11 P–K4 P–QR3 12 P–K5 N–R4 13 B–K3 P–QN4** If 13 . . . P×P 14 P–R5 undermining Black's QB4 is very strong. **14 P–N3 P×BP 15 P×P B–N5!** Forcing White to release tension in the centre. **16 P×P P×P 17 R–R3**

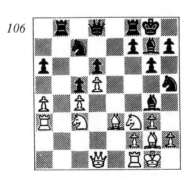

The position is level and was soon agreed drawn.

Black Plays . . . P–K3 (or . . . P–K4) and White Plays P×P(ep)
Portisch–Honfi   Hungarian Championship 1962
1 P–Q4 N–KB3 2 P–QB4 P–KN3 3 N–KB3 B–N2 4 P–KN3 0–0 5 B–N2

P–Q3 6 0–0 P–B4 7 P–Q5 P–K3 8 P×P White would also play this against
7 ... P–K4 **8 ... B×P** The Q pawn is weak after 8 ... P×P **9 N–N5!** The
immediate assault on the Q pawn by 9 B–B4 is not so good because of 9
... B×P or even 9 ... P–Q4. **9 ... N–B3** White threatened 10 B×P.
**10 N×B P×N 11 N–B3 Q–B2 12 B–B4 QR–Q1 13 Q–Q2 R–Q2 14 QR–Q1
KR–Q1**

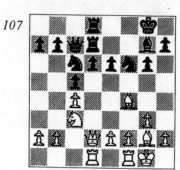

107

White stands better since Black's pieces are tied to the defence of his
Q pawn.

The move order in the previous extract is important. If White had
played 6 N–QB3 (also a common move) instead of 6 0–0 then after 6 ...
P–B4 7 P–Q5 P–K3 8 P×P? B×P 9 N–N5 B×P 10 B×P QN–Q2 and Black
has good compensation for the sacrificed material after either 11 Q×P
R–N1 or 11 B×R Q×B 12 0–0 P–Q4. This variation does not work for
Black after 6 0–0 in view of the line 6 ... P–B4 7 P–Q5 P–K3 8 P×P
B×P 9 N–N5 B×P 10 B×P N–Q2 11 N–R3! and Black's bishop on ...
QB5 has no good retreat square. Black therefore has to play 11 ... R–N1
12 N×B R×B 13 N×QP with inadequate compensation for the pawn.

After 6 N–B3 P–B4 7 P–Q5 P–K3 White should therefore play 8 0–0
transposing into a Modern Benoni Defence after 8 ... P×P 9 P×P.

Donner–Penrose   Flushing 1966
**1 P–Q4 N–KB3 2 P–QB4 P–KN3 3 N–KB3 B–N2 4 P–KN3 0–0 5 B–N2
P–Q3 6 0–0 N–B3 7 N–B3 P–QR3 8 P–Q5 N–QR4 9 N–Q2** Threatening
10 P–QN4 trapping the knight on R4. **9 ... P–B4 10 Q–B2** The immediate
10 P–N3 loses a pawn after 10 ... N×QP. **10 ... R–N1 11 P–N3 P–QN4
12 B–N2 P–K3 13 P×KP** If White plays non-committally by 13 QR–N1
Black should reply 13 ... R–K1 threatening 14 ... P×QP 15 BP×P (Not
15 N×QP? R×P) transposing into a Modern Benoni type of position. The
immediate 13 ... P×QP is not so good in view of 14 N×QP and White's
control of the square Q5 guarantees him some advantage. **13 ... P×KP**
13 ... B×P ceding control of ... Q4 is not so good. Compare the previous

note. **14 PXP PXP 15 N(B)-K4 B-N2 16 QR-Q1 Q-K2 17 NXN+ BXN 18 BXKB RXB 19 N-K4 BXN 20 BXB**

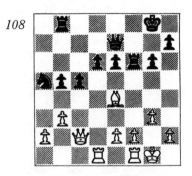

108

Both sides have played accurately and the chances are about level.

Black Plays ... P-K4 and White does not Capture

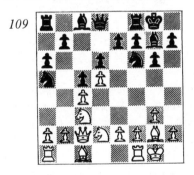

109

Petrosian-Spassky   World Championship 1966

From Diagram 109 play continued **10 ... P-K4 11 P-N3** 11 PXP ep would reach the sort of position which arises after ... P-K3, PXP considered in the previous extract **11 ... N-N5** Preparing ... P-B4. **12 P-K4** If 12 P-KR3 the black knight is quite well placed after 12 ... N-R3. It will ultimately re-enter the fray via KB2 or KB4. **12 ... P-B4 13 PXP** This is normally the correct response to ... P-B4. Black obtains a dangerous attack on the kingside if he is allowed to play ... P-B5. In some similar positions White can himself play P-B4 instead of PXP. In the present position however, 13 P-B4? would lose to 13 ... N-K6, **13 ... PXP.** 13 ... BXP? would be a positional blunder (as so often in similar positions in the King's Indian Defence) since it gives White a wonderful square for his pieces on K4. **14 N-Q1?** (14 B-N2!) **14 ... P-N4!** If White had not obligingly retreated his knight Black would have had to have wasted time preparing this move by ... R-N1 or B–N2. **15 P–B3 P–K5! 16 B–N2 KP×P 17 B×P B×B 18 Q×B N–K4 19 B–K2 P–B5?** After 19 . . . R–R2!, preparing to transfer the rook to the kingside, Black would have a clear advantage. **20 P×BP B–R6?** This second mistake gives White a chance to score a glorious victory. Correct was 20 . . . R×P and if 21 R×R Q–N4+ leading to a complicated position with about even chances.

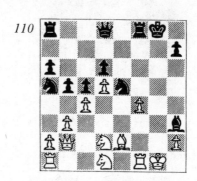

110

21 N–K3!! B×R 22 R×B N–N3 23 B–N4 N×KBP 24 R×N! R×R 25 B–K6+ R–B2 26 N–K4 Q–R5 27 N×QP Q–N4+ 28 K–R1 R–R2 29 B×R+ R×B 30 Q–R8+!! 1–0.

This game illustrates the double-edged nature of the positions which arise after . . . P–K4. Black can obtain a very strong attack but he runs the risk that his own king will become exposed.

. . . P–B4 Exchange Variation

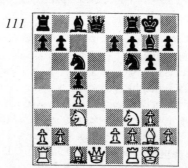

111

Diagram 121 can arise after the move **1 P–Q4 N–KB3 2 P–QB4 P–KN3 3 N–KB3 B–N2 4 P–KN3 0–0 5 B–N2 P–Q3 6 0–0 P–B4 7 N–B3 (or 7 P×P) N–B3 8 P×P P×P**

It is a common fallacy that symmetrical positions are easy for Black to draw. It is true that such positions are normally drawn but it is important that Black should realise that his task is not easy. The correct antidote is normally for Black to break the symmetry as soon as possible so that the significance of White's first move is reduced.

From Diagram 111 Keene gives the following analysis, **9 B–K3 B–K3**. Black could also break the symmetry at once by 9 . . . Q–R4 or 9 . . . N–Q2; **10 B×P Q–R4**. Now Black must break the symmetry. White obtains the advantage after 10 . . . B×P 11 Q–R4 B–R3 (11 . . . Q–R4?? 12 Q×B) 12 KR–Q1. **11 B–QR3 KR–Q1 12 N–Q2 N–KN5 13 N–Q5 KN–K4 14 P–B4 N×P 15 N×N Q–N4 16 N(B)–K3 B–Q5.**

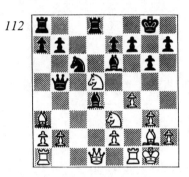

The position is unclear. This variation may not represent best play by either side but it does illustrate how rapidly a symmetrical position can be transformed into a position in which each side has winning chances.

Black Plays . . . P–B4 and . . . P×P

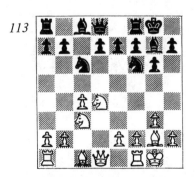

Diagram 113 arises after **1 P–Q4 N–KB3 2 P–QB4 P–KN3 3 N–KB3 B–N2 4 P–KN3 0–0 5 B–N2 P–B4 6 0–0 P×P 7 N×P N–B3 8 N–B3.**

White has a significant space advantage which should give him the better chances. His aim is to consolidate before Black can obtain sufficient counterplay by attacking White's B4 pawn or by playing . . . P–QN4.

Donner–Pomar   Brunnen 1966

From Diagram 113 play continued **8 . . . N×N. 8 . . . P–Q3** is a dubious pawn sacrifice. If **8 . . . Q–B2 9 P–B5!** cramps Black further. **9 Q×N P–Q3**

10 Q–Q3 B–B4 If at once **10 . . . B–K3 11 B×P.** So Black sacrifices a tempo to induce White to block the KR1–QR8 diagonal. **11 P–K4 B–K3 12 P–QN3 Q–R4 13 B–Q2** Not 13 B–N2 N×KP! **13 . . . Q–R4 14 P–B3 B–R6 15 QR–B1 B×B 16 K×B KR–Q1 17 KR–Q1 B–R3 18 N–Q5 N×N 19 BP×N**

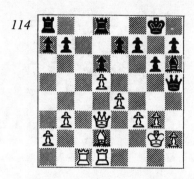

114

White has consolidated his space advantage and he eventually won by penetrating down the QB file.

Black does not Play . . . P–B4

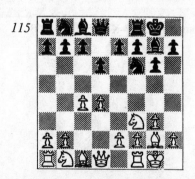

115

Diagram 115 can arise after the moves **1 P–Q4 N–KB3 2 P–QB4 P–KN3 3 N–KB3 B–N2 4 P–KN3 0–0 5 B–N2 P–Q3 6 0–0**

In the previous chapter we considered positions in which Black played . . . QN–Q2 and . . . P–K4. So far in the present chapter we have considered positions in which Black plays . . . P–B4, either at once or after 6 . . .

N–B3 7 N–B3 P–QR3 8 P–Q5 N–QR4 9 N–Q2. We now briefly consider alternative plans for Black.

Black Plays 6 . . . P–B3

6 . . . P–B3 often transposes into variations already considered, e.g. 7 N–B3 QN–Q2 8 P–K4 P–K4 or 7 N–B3 Q–R4 8 P–KR3 (if 8 P–K4 B–N5 equalises) 8 . . . P–K4 9 P–K4 QN–Q2. Three independent lines deserve a mention.
(a) 6 . . . P–B3 7 N–B3 P–QR3 8 P–K4 (8 P–QR4 preventing . . . P–QN4 is not) only unnecessary but also bad. Black plays 8 . . . P–QR4! followed by . . . N–R3 and . . . N–QN5 entrenching his knight on an aggressive square.) 8 . . . P–QN4 9 P–K5.

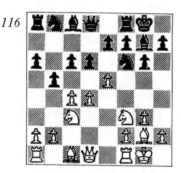

116

White's expansion in the centre is more significant than Black's on the queenside.
(b) 6 . . . P–B3 7 N–B3 B–N5 Black prefaces this move by . . . P–B3 since the immediate 6 . . . B–N5 is dubious in view of 7 Q–N3 intending to answer either 7 . . . P–N3 or 7 . . . Q–B1 by 8 N–K5 with complications which probably favour White. 8 P–KR3 B×N 9 B×B.

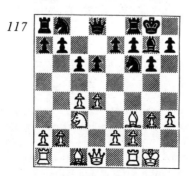

117

White has forced Black to carry out his plan of exchanging bishop for knight. But it is doubtful whether this plan was worth carrying out! White stands a little better.

(c) 6 . . . P-B3 7 N-B3 B-B4. Black tries to impede P-K4. 8 N-KR4! B-K3
Other retreats by the bishop allow P-K4. 9 P-Q5 PXP 10 PXP B-Q2 11
B-K3 Q-R4 12 B-Q4

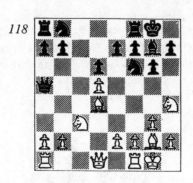

118

White has a useful space advantage.

Black Plays 6 . . . N-B3 Without a Later . . . P-B4
After 6 . . . N-B3 the play often transposes into lines already considered
by 7 N-B3 P-QR3 8 P-Q5 N-QR4 9 N-Q2 P-B4. Other possibilities are
a) 6 . . . N-B3 7 N-B3 P-K4 8 P-Q5 N-K2

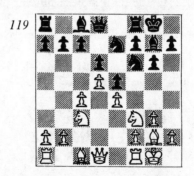

119

This position has the same strategic features as Diagram 60. The only
significant difference is that White has fianchettoed his king's bishop
rather than played it to e2. This makes it more difficult for Black to
pursue his kingside attack. As in Diagram 60 White can play on the queenside by, e.g. 9 P-QN4 intending N-Q3 and P-B4.
b) 6 . . . N-B3 7 N-B3 B-N5 8 P-Q5 BXN (It may be better for Black to
play 8 . . . N-QR4 followed by 9 . . . P-B4 but in that case his bishop is
misplaced on N5.) 9 PXB N-QR4 10 Q-K2

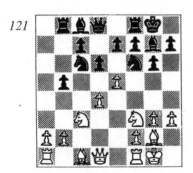

White has a slight plus. He has the bishop pair and chances of attacking Black's K pawn. His doubled pawns are not weak and it may be possible to use the front B pawn to attack Black's kingside by P-B4-B5.

c) 6 . . . N-B3 7 N-B3 P-QR3 8 P-KR3. 8 P-Q5 N-QR4 9 N-Q2 P-B4 leads to lines already considered, 8 . . . R-N1 9 P-K4. 9 B-K3 is also possible, e.g. 9 . . . P-QN4 10 P×P P×P 11 N-Q2 N-QR4 12 P-QN4 with a slight edge. 9 . . . P-QN4. 9 . . . P-K4 is also possible though White stands a little better after 10 B-K3. 10 P×P P×P 11 P-K5

The position becomes very complicated after either 11 . . . P×P 12 P×P N-Q2 13 P-K6 or 11 . . . N-Q2 12 N-N5 threatening both 13 B×N and 13 P-K6. White probably has the better chances.

9 The Modern Benoni

The Modern Benoni is not a variation of the King's Indian Defence. It is a completely separate opening but one in which Black's set-up has many characteristics in common with King's Indian formations: The K-side structure; the pawns at Q3 and QB4 rubbing shoulders with White's QP on Q5. The following position shows the basic Benoni set-up, from Black's point of view.

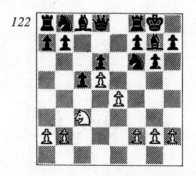

122

White's KP sometimes remains on K2 during the early part of the game, in which case the white KB is put into fianchetto, but later if he is to achieve anything, White must advance his KP to K4 and eventually to K5.

The first thing that becomes apparent on examining the above position is the way in which it is unbalanced. White has a central pawn majority of 2:1 and a majority of 4:3 on the right half of the board. Black has a 3:2 Q-side majority. White will therefore base his strategy on a central breakthrough and/or a K-side attack. Black's counterplay will combine a Q-side pawn advance with pressure along the half-open K-file. Let us now look at two examples that illustrate these strategies.

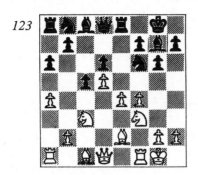

123

Hollis–Kondali   Correspondence 1972

White has contained Black's Q-side ambitions by means of P–QR4 whereas Black has not been able to exercise sufficient control over his K4 square. As a result there followed: **13 P–K5! PXP 14 PXP N–N5 15 B–KN5 P–B3 16 PXP BXP 17 Q–Q2 B–B4 18 P–R3! BXB 19 QXB N–K6 20 QXQ RXQ 21 R–B2 P–KR4 22 N–R4 R–KB1 23 R–K1 N–B7 24 R(K)–KB1 N–K6 25 NXP!** Resigns. Even after queens were exchanged Black was unable to resist the pressure on his K-side.

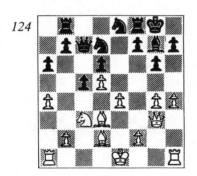

124

Haggquist–Polugayevsky   Reykjavik 1957

Black has the . . . K4 square well under control (queen at . . . QB2, knight at . . . Q2, bishop at . . . KN2 plus the all important pawn at . . . Q3). White will not be able to achieve anything with P–K5 so he has put all his eggs into a direct assault on the enemy king, neglecting his Q-side in the process. Young Polugayevsky was not slow to seize the initiative: **16 . . . P–B5 17 B–B2 P–QN4 18 PXP PXP 19 P–R5 P–N5 20 N–Q1 N–K4** suddenly White's forces are retreating and Black's are advancing. **21 P–B4 P–B6 22 PXP N–B5 23 P–K5** Too late! **23 . . . NXB 24 RPXP BPXP 25 KXN Q–B5 26 Q–R3 QXKBPch 27 N–K3 PXPch 28 K–Q3 P–R3 29 P–N5 R–N5 30 Q–K6ch K–R1 31 QR–Q1 R–Q5ch 32 KXP QXNch 33 R–Q3**

R×Rch **34 B×R N–B2 35 Q×NP B×Pch** 36 Resigns. Once Black achieved ... P–QN4 his attack played itself.

Having seen these examples we are now able to define the basic strategy of each player.

White's Basic Strategy

Prevent the advance ... P–QN4, which means:

a) playing P–QR4 (and if Black answers or has played ... P–QR3 but not ... P–QN3, advancing P–QR5).

b) controlling QN5 with the QB3 knight and possibly the queen or bishop on the KB1–QR6 diagonal.

Building up for the critical advance P–K5, which means supporting the K5 square as many times as possible.

Black's Basic Strategy

Trying to force ... P–QN4.

Trying to prevent P–K5, which means keeping control of the ... K4 square.

Let us now look at some concrete ideas for both players.

Ideas for White

1) Playing P–QR4 and meeting ... P–QR3 with P–R5
2) Preparing the advance P–K5 with P–KB4
3) Supporting P–K5 with pieces only, not with the KBP.
4) Playing P–KB4 followed by P–K5 QP×P; P–KB5, to attack the black king.

White Plays P–QR4 and Meets ... P–QR3 with P–R5

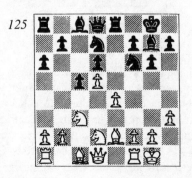

125

Bukić–Velimirović   Yugoslav Championship 1965

Black has just played 11 ... P–QR3, intending 12 ... P–QN4, and so **12 P–QR4 R–QN1** again threatening ... P–QN4. **13 P–R5** Now Black cannot obtain a pawn duo on QN4 and QB4 since . . . P-QN4 is met by P×P e.p. leaving Black with an isolated QRP (sometimes however, this push is Black's only way to stay in the game). **13 . . . Q-B2 14 Q-B2 P-QN4** Otherwise Black will be squashed by P-B4 and a slow build up to P-K5. **15 P×P ep N×NP 16 N-N3! Q-K2 17 N-R5** This move highlights one of the disadvantages that Black faces after . . . P-QN4; P×P ep His QB3 square is open for invasion. With pawns on . . . QN4 and . . . QB4 However Black controls all the squares via which White's minor pieces can penetrate. **17 . . . B-Q2 18 N-B6 B×N 19 P×B.** The two bishops and the weakness of the Black QR pawn now give White a clear advantage.

White Prepares the Advance P-K5 with P-KB4

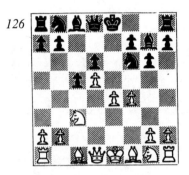

126

Kuzmin-Espig   Zinnowitz 1971

We have seen one example of this theme on page 93. The present position is, in fact, part of a variation whose strategy is based entirely on the early advance of the KP to the fifth rank. **8 P-K5** Although he is lagging behind in development, White hopes that the disruption caused in Black's game will compensate. This advance produces positions of the type that can arise in the Four Pawns Attack (see chapter 2). **8 . . . P×P?** Black should not allow the position to be opened up in this way. After 8 . . . KN-Q2 he has good chances of defending successfully. **9 P×P KN-Q2 10 P-K6 P×P 11 P×P N-KB3** It looks tempting to exchange queens by 11 . . . Q-R5ch 12 P-N3 B×Nch 13 P×B Q-K5ch 14 Q-K2 Q×Qch 15 B×Q, but although he wins a pawn Black cannot survive the pressure along several open lines. **12 Q×Qch** If Black had not exchanged pawns at move 8 White would be denied this possibility. **12 . . . K×Q 13 B-KN5 B×P 14 0-0-0ch K-K2 15 R-K1 K-B2 16 N-R3 R-K1 17 N-B4 B-B4 18 B-B4ch K-B1 19 R×Rch N×R 20 R-B1 B-B3 21 B×B N×B 22 N-K6ch** Resigns. If the king moves, 23 N-B7 follows. The fact that White won so easily here despite his lag in development should serve as a warning of the potential in a properly supported P-K5 attack.

White Supports P–K5 with only his Pieces

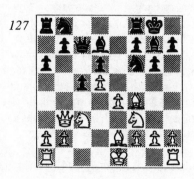

127

Portisch–Fischer   Palma Interzonal 1970
Black's queen is overworked, protecting both Q3 and QN2. Portisch takes
advantage of the situation with **12 P–K5! P×P 13 B×KP Q–B1 14 0–0
B–N5 15 P–KR3 B×N 16 B×B QN–Q2 17 B–Q6** White has a big advantage
in space and Fischer was somewhat fortunate to survive with a draw.

White Plays P–KB4, followed by P–K5 QP×P; P–B5

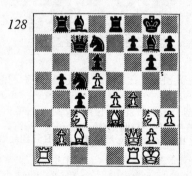

128

Penrose–Tal   Leipzig Olympiad 1960
White wants to open up the KB-file but an immediate P–B5 can be met by
. . . N–K4 when Black's knight is beautifully placed. So **19 P–K5! P×P 20
P–B5** The point. Now Black cannot make use of his K4 square. **20 . . .
B–N2 21 QR–Q1 B–QR1 22 N(B3)–K4 N–R5 23 B×N P×B 24 P×P BP×P
25 Q–B7ch K–R1 26 N–QB5 Q–R2 27 Q×N Q×Q 28 N×Q R×P 29 N–N6
R–N6 30 N×BP and White soon won.**

Ideas for Black
The key to Black's counterplay lies in the advance of his QNP and it is
therefore important that we examine the various ways this may be achieved.

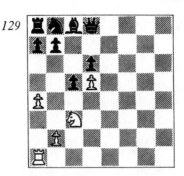

Here we see the typical Q-side Modern Benoni setup. White's QB3 knight and his QRP are both placed to prevent ... P-QN4 by Black. In addition, White often has a bishop on K2 or Q3, from where it can perform the same function. How can Black support this advance?

There are various manoeuvres which, by themselves or in combination can help to make ... P-QN4 a viable proposition for Black.

1) Black Plays ... P-QR3

We have already seen examples of White playing P-QR4, before or after Black's ... P-QR3. This inhibits ... P-QN4 not only because the pawn on QN4 might be *en prise* but also because the exchange of pawns, RP×P RP×P, leaves Black's QR hanging. Black must therefore make sure, before playing ... P-QN4, that either his QR moves (usually to QN1 to support the pawn advance) or that it is protected, as happens when both the QN and QB have moved off the first rank.

If White plays P-QR4 before Black's ... P-QR3 Black must be alert to the possibility of P-R5 as a response to ... P-QR3. The effects of P-R5 have been seen in the Bukić-Velimirović example on page 94.

In order to avoid the cramping effect of P-R5, Black sometimes meets P-QR4 with ... P-QN3. Then, if White does play P-R5, Black will be able to advance his QNP without allowing the *en passant* capture which leaves his QRP isolated and his QB3 square weak. Although the manoeuvre ... P-QN3, ... P-QR3, ... P-QN4 takes longer to get a black pawn established on QN4, the sacrifice of a tempo is often worthwhile. ... P-QN3 also allows the freeing exchange that will follow ... B-QR3, and so it is a dual purpose move.

2) Black Plays ... N-QR3 and ... N-B2

If Black's knight is not needed on Q2 to prevent the advance of the white KP, it can be used on QB2 to support the advance of the QNP. Obviously, if Black is going to carry out this manoeuvre, he must do so before playing ... P-QR3.

3) Black Plays ... R–QN1

This rook move leaves White in control of the QR-file after the pawn exchange on ... QN4, but it is not usually serious from Black's point of view because often he can switch his rook back to the QR-file after his QNP has been established on ... QN4 or ... QN5.

We shall now look at three examples of these manoeuvres.

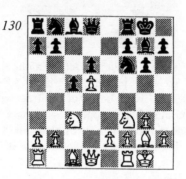

130

Bertok–Matulović   Sochi 1966

9 ... N–R3 10 P–KR3 N–B2 11 P–QR4 Unnecessary, White could play 11 P–K4 since 11 ... P–QN4 allows 12 P–K5! and if 12 ... P×P? 13 P–Q6 wins material. **11 ... R–K1 12 N–Q2 P–N3 13 N–B4 B–QR3 14 Q–N3 B×N 15 Q×B P–QR3 16 B–N5 P–KR3 17 B–Q2 Q–Q2** This is often a useful move, uniting the rooks and supporting ... QN4. **18 P–K4 P–QN4** Black has achieved his aim and the chances are equal.

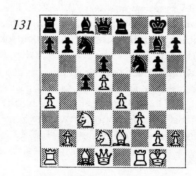

131

Gligorić–Matulović   Belgrade 1969

12 ... P–N3 13 N–B4 B–QR3 14 B–N5 P–R3 15 B–Q2 B×N 16 B×B P–QR3 17 K–R1 N–Q2 18 R–QN1 R–N1 19 Q–K2 Q–B1 20 P–QN4 P–QN4! with equal chances.

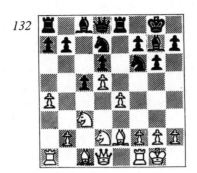

132

Larsen–Ljubojević　　　　　　　　　　　　　　　　　Milan 1975

11 ... P-QR3 Black does not fear 12 P-R5 because after 12 ... P-QN4 13 PXP ep NXNP, White cannot invade Black's QB3 square. **12 K-R1 R-N1 13 P-B4 P-B5! 14 P-K5!** If 14 BXP N-B4 (Threatening the KP) 15 Q-B2 N-N5 16 N-B3 BXN, and Black restores the material equilibrium while keeping the more active game. **14 ... PXP 15 NXP P-QN4! 16 RPXP RPXP**, with chances for both sides in the lively struggle ahead.

Finally, it should be mentioned that although the move ... B-Q2 also supports ... QN4 it is rarely good. Black usually gets a cramped game after ... B-Q2, his QP is deprived more vulnerable and the square ... Q2 is deprived to his knights. The correct role for Black's QB in the Modern Benoni is to be exchanged off for one of White's minor pieces, either via ... P-QN3 and ... B-QR3, or via ... B-KN5.

Keeping Control over ... K4

It has already been stated that while Black is striving for ... P-QN4 he must also take care not to allow White to play P-K5 under favourable circumstances. This means that Black must keep control over his K4 square and try to reduce White's support of P-K5. There are various ways in which this can be accomplished:

1) Playing ... R-K1. From this square the rook protects ... K4 and exerts some pressure on the white KP.

2) Playing ... Q-B2. This move indirectly supports ... K4, but Black must be alert to the possibility of N-QN5 by White, which means that ... Q-B2 is normally played after Black has guarded against N-QN5 with ... P-QR3.

3) Playing ... QN-Q2 or ... KN-Q2. From Q2 Black's knight protects ... K4 and if it is the KN which goes to Q2, ... K4 receives the added support of the ... KN2 bishop.

4) Exchanging off White's KB3 knight to reduce the pressure on ... K4. This can often be accomplished by ... B-KN5, though White can, in some

variations, meet . . . B-KN5 with N(KB3)-Q2, and then play N-QB4 from where the knight still supports K5.

5) Exchanging off White's QB4 knight. If White plays N-KB3-Q2-QB4 before the black QB has moved, Black can play . . . P-QN3 and . . . B-QR3, to exchange off this knight and thereby reduce the pressure that White exerts on K5. When considering this manoeuvre Black must take into account the possibility of P-QR4 (in reply to . . . P-QN3) and N-QN5 (in reply to . . . B-QR3), since the exchange . . . B(QR3)×N(QN4); RP×B, leaves Black's Q-side cramped unless he can do something about White's newly arrived pawn on QN5.

Here is an example in which Black puts more than one of these ideas into operation.

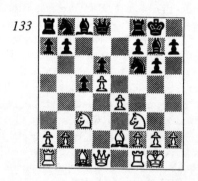

133

Taimanov–Stein   U.S.S.R. Championship 1971

9 . . . P-QR3 10 P-QR4 B-KN5 11 B-KB4 R-K1 Not only keeping an eye on . . . K4 but also threatening the white KP. **12 Q-B2 Q-B2** Safe, since White cannot play N-QN5. **13 P-R3 B×N** Black does not object to conceding the bishop pair because he reduces White's pressure on K5. **14 B×B QN-Q2 15 P-R5 R-K2 16 P-KN4 P-R3 17 B-N2 QR-K1 18 B-N3 N-R2 19 N-N1 P-KN4 20 N-Q2 N-K4** This was the point of . . . P-KN4; White cannot drive away the knight with P-B4. **21 R-R4 N-B1 22 P-B4 P×P 23 R×P N(B1)-N3 24 R-B1 Q-Q1 25 R-R3 R-B2** Having secured complete domination of . . . K4, Black now commences his Q-side counterattack. **26 R-N3 N-R5 27 R-N6 P-B5 28 Q-R4 R-KB1 29 Q-R3 R-B4 30 B-B2 R-N4 31 R×QP Q-K2 32 R-N6 Q×Q 33 P×Q N×B 34 R×R P×R 35 K×N R-R1 36 B-N6 N-Q2 37 B-B7 B-B6 38 N-B3 B×P** Black has recovered his pawn and his Q-side pawn majority gives him a clear advantage. **39 B-Q6 N-B3 40 B-K7 N×KP 41 N-Q4 P-N5 42 P×P B-N3 43 R-B4 R-R7ch 44 K-B3 N-Q7ch 45 K-K3 N-N6 46 B-B5 N×B 47 P×N B×P 48 K-B3 R-QN7 49 R-K4 P-N4** and the advance of the Q-side pawns proved decisive.

The Golden Rules of the Modern Benoni

1) As White, prevent . . . P–QN4 for as long as possible.

2) As White, try to build up to the advance P–K5.

3) As Black, play for a Q-side counterattack based on . . . P–QN4.

4) As Black, keep control over . . . K4 and try to exchange off White's KB3 knight.

10 The Benko Gambit

In the previous chapter, on Benoni positions, we examined formations in which White has a pawn at Q5 but no QBP, and Black has pawns at Q3 and QB4. In Benoni positions Black tries to achieve Q-side counterplay by forcing the move ... P-QN4 and White attempts to inhibit this move with P-QR4. More often than not Black experiences great difficulty in forcing ... P-QN4 under favourable circumstances.

In this chapter we shall look at a relatively new opening, The Benko Gambit, in which Black plays ... P-QN4 as early as move 3. This move offers the sacrifice of a pawn in return for which Black gets enormous counterplay.

One important structural difference between the positions discussed in this chapter and Benoni formations is that here Black's KP has not moved, and so Black's QP is not vulnerable and his KB3 square can not be subjected to the same sort of pressure.

The Benko Gambit represents the most important contribution to opening theory for three decades or more. Here is a defence (counterattack) which gives Black the initiative from the very beginning of the game and in which this initiative frequently lasts right through the middle game and well into the ending. Black has four lines of attack in the Benko Gambit; the QR and QN-files, and the KR1-QR8 and KB1-QR6 diagonals. White has no equivalent attacking possibility—his sole aggressive motif is the advance of the K-pawn to K5, but this advance is not easy to achieve and even when it is played it is often of limited or no effect.

In return for all this Black sacrifices only one pawn, and a wing pawn at that. Not even a Slater or a Rothschild could ask for a better return on such a small investment.

The basic positions in the two main variations of the Benko Gambit are shown in the following diagrams. These positions will help the reader in his understanding of the principle motifs and ideas in the gambit.

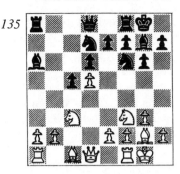

From these two positions we can see the role that will be played by each of Black's pieces as the game develops. His rooks will put pressure on White's Q-side pawns from QR1 and QN1, occasionally doubling on one of these files to intensify the pressure against one of the pawns. Black's KN2 bishop augments the pressure against White's QN2 pawn, while his QR3 bishop exerts pressure along the diagonal to KB8. If the light squared bishops are exchanged (as was the case in Diagram 134) Black will often renew his pressure along the QR3–KB8 diagonal by bringing his queen to QR3 via QR4, QN3 or QB1.

Black's knights can serve two distinct functions. They can act as aggressors, adding to the pressure on White's Q-side from QB5 or, when White's K-pawn has moved, from Q6; or they can be employed to exchange off White's knights by manoeuvres such as ... N-KN5-K4 (to exchange off the White KB3 knight) and ... N-QR3-QB2-QN4 (or ... N-K1-QB2-QN4 or ... N-Q2-QN3-QR5) to exchange off the white QB3 knight. The reader might at first be surprised to learn that the exchange of pieces is one of Black's aims in the Benko Gambit but it is the great paradox of this gambit that even though he is a pawn down Black's position usually improves with each exchange of pieces and that Benko Gambit endings (especially major piece endings) tend to favour Black.

Black's queen also has an aggressive role in the Benko Gambit, sometimes adding to the pressure on White's Q-side pawns from QR4 or QN3 and sometimes creating play on the QR3–KB8 diagonal after the exchange of light squared bishops. Nevertheless, Black should not be afraid to exchange queens because even in their absence his Q-side pressure is normally of a lasting nature.

With so many dynamic possibilities at his disposal Black has by far the easier position to play. White, on the other hand, must be extremely careful lest the pressure on one of his Q-side pawns should become overwhelming, and in particular White should watch out for combinative possibilities on his QN2 square. The most sensible way for White to play against the Benko Gambit is to try to consolidate his position and to set up pawns on QN3 and QR4 (if possible with a knight on QN5 as well). If he can create and maintain this structure without succumbing to a tactical stroke such as ... P-QB5, White will have excellent winning prospects in the ending.

Before we enter into a detailed discussion of the most typical Benko Gambit motifs, let us first confirm the endgame paradox by examining two endings in which Black is a pawn down but with the better chances.

136

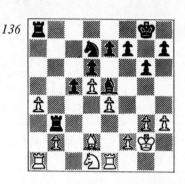

Kuzmin–Georgadze   ½-final 40th U.S.S.R. Ch 1972

Black is about to win back his sacrificed pawn because he not only attacks QN7 but also threatens ... N–N3 followed by ... N–B5. So White tries to simplify. **20 R–K3 B✕QNP 21 R–R2** If 21 R✕R B✕R 22 R–N7 (or 22 P–R5 K–B1) 22 ... N–B3 23 R✕P R✕P, and Black's passed QB-pawn will eventually prove decisive. **21 ... R✕R 22 N✕R Ḅ–Q5 23 N–B4 P–B4!** The thematic break in endings with this particular pawn structure (white pawns on K4 and Q5 v black pawns on QB4, Q3 and K2). Either White exchanges on KB5 leaving himself with an isolated Q-pawn or White plays P–KB3 allowing ... BP✕P, BP✕P and Black will eventually pick up the K5 pawn. In endings of this type White's central pawn structure will always collapse in the face of the march of Black's king to K4. **24 P✕P P✕P 25 B–N5 K–B2 26 P–B4 R–QN1!** **27 N–R5** Or 27 P–R5 R–N5 28 P–R6 R✕N 29 P–R7 N–N3 winning. **27 ... P–R3!!** **28 B✕RP** If 28 B–R4 B–B3 29 N–B6 R–QR1, and after the exchange of bishops Black will go for White's Q5 pawn. **28 ... N–N3 29 N–B6 R–QR1 30 P–N4 N✕QP 31 N✕B P✕N 32 P–R5 K–N3 33 B–N5 P–K4! 34 P–R6 N–K6+! 35 K–N1 P–K5 36 B–K7 P–Q6 37 B✕P N–B7! 38 P✕P+ K–B2 39 R–N2 P–Q7 40 R–N7+ K–N1** 0–1. White's QR-pawn could always be stopped.

137

Mecking–Szabo — Buenos Aires 1970

31 P-R5 This pawn soon becomes indefensible. **31 ... R-N4 32 Q-B4 R-R1 33 P-QN4 R×RP 34 Q×Q R(4)×Q 35 R×R R×R 36 R-K2 N×KP! 37 P×P P×P 38 R×N R×N+ 39 K-B3 R-R6+ 40 K-N2 K-B1** Black is now a pawn up and the win is not difficult. **41 R-B4 R-R4 42 K-B3 K-K1 43 P-B5 P×P 44 K-B4 K-Q2 45 K×P K-Q3** The white Q-pawn is ripe. **46 R-KR4 K×P 47 R×P K-Q5 48 K-N4 R-R3 49 R-R8 P-B5 50 K-B3 K-Q6** 0-1 The QB-pawn cannot be stopped.

Black's advantage in Benko Gambit endings lies partly in the fact that once White's QN-pawn has disappeared Black has a protected passed QB-pawn, and partly in the ease with which his king can attack White's central pawn mass by marching to ... K4. With the major pieces on the board Black cannot afford to put his king in jeopardy but despite this he usually has the better endgame prospects because White's space advantage can rebound on him, acting like a vacuum sucking Black's pieces into the white position.

Now that we have seen how Black should play a typical Benko Gambit ending we can take a detailed look at the most frequently recurring motifs in the middle game. Remember that Black's basic strategy is to build up pressure on White's QR and QN-pawns, to prevent White from establishing a safe structure on QN3 and QR4 to exchange pieces whenever possible, and finally to reach a favourable endgame. White's basic strategy is to consolidate his extra pawn by supporting and strengthening his Q-side, establishing pawns on QR4 and QN3, limiting Black's counterplay, and eventually to neutralize Black's initiative and emerge with a safe extra pawn.

Black Exchanges Knights by . . . N–KN5–K4
One of Black's easiest tasks to accomplish is the exchange of knights.

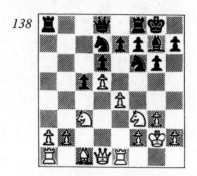

138

1 . . . N–N5 2 P–KR3 This move is often played in response to . . . N–KN5 but it is not always logical. After all, since Black's knight is aiming to move to . . . K4 in any event, why waste a tempo to encourage it on its way? **2 . . . N(5)–K4 3 N×N** If the knight retreats White has a very passive position. **3 . . . N×N 4 P–B4 N–Q2 5 Q–B2 Q–N3 6 R–Q2 P–B5** Black has succeeded in exchanging a pair of knights and he now has the more dynamic position . . . N–B4 and . . . N–Q6 will soon be possible.

Black Exchanges Knights by . . . N–QN3–R5

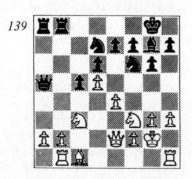

139

1 . . . N–N3 Heading for . . . QR5. **2 B–Q2 N–R5 3 N×N** If 3 P–R3 N×N 4 B×N Q–R5, attacking the K-pawn and keeping the move . . . R–N6 in reserve. **3 . . . Q×N** White cannot defend both the QR2 pawn and the K4 pawn and so his position will soon collapse. This example is rather dramatic but it does demonstrate the importance of White's QB3 knight and how difficult life can become for White once this knight has been exchanged off.

Black has a Knight at . . . Q6

We have already stated that knights can also adopt an aggressive role in the Benko Gambit. The ideal square for a black knight is . . . Q6 (once White's K-pawn has advanced) and so Black must first support the . . . Q6 square (either by . . . P-QB5 or by putting his queen or bishop on the QR3-KB8 diagonal). Once Black establishes a knight on . . . Q6 he will usually have at least a slight advantage.

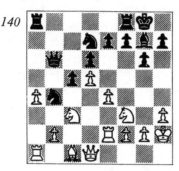

140

Trapl-Knaak   Sombor 1972

15 . . . P-B5 16 B-K3 N-B4 17 N-Q2 N(N)-Q6 Already White is quite lost. **18 N×P Q-N5 19 B×N Q×N 20 B-R3** Forced, otherwise 20 . . . N×NP is crushing. **20 . . . P-B4!** Now that White's K-side has become weakened by lack of protection Black opens up another front. **21 P×P R×BP 22 Q-B2 B-K4+ 23 P-N3 N×BP 24 R×B P×R 25 B×P N-Q6 26 P-N3 Q-Q5 27 N-Q1 N-K8 28 Q-B4** and 0-1 (28 . . . Q-Q7+).

Black Plays a Combination on . . . QN7

We saw in the above example how a black knight on . . . Q6 introduces all sorts of tactical possibilities based on capturing the . . . QN7 pawn. In fact most of the combinations played in the Benko Gambit begin with the capture on . . . QN7. Here is one example—there are dozens of others which equally well illustrate the vulnerability of White's QN2.

141

Vaiser–Georgadze U.S.S.R. Young Masters Ch 1973

15 . . . R×P! 16 Q×R B×N 17 Q–N7 Q–R2!! Black attacks so many pieces that he is assured of recouping all his investment. **18 Q×Q** If 18 Q–B6 P–B3 19 QR–N1 B×R 20 R–N7 Q–R5 21 R×N Q×Q 22 P×Q B–R4! and the white QB-pawn will soon fall. **18 . . . R×Q 19 N–Q2** If 19 B×P B×R(R8) 20 R×B P–B3 and the white bishop has no way to escape. **19 . . . B×R 20 R×B P–B3**. The combination is over and Black has won back the pawn. Black now has all the usual advantages of the typical Benko Gambit ending (protected passed QB-pawn, more active pieces, etc.) and the game was won by Black after a lengthy and stubborn defence by his opponent.

By now we hope that we have convinced the reader that the Benko Gambit is a most potent and dynamic weapon against 1 P–Q4, but just in case we have done my job too well and persuaded someone that 1 P–Q4 loses out of hand, we shall now give some examples of a successful strategy being employed by White (or rather what happens when Black defends badly).

White Advances Quickly with P–K5

142

This position stems from one of the most recent weapons in the anti-Benko armoury—a system in which White strives for the advance P–K5 from the earliest stages of the game. **10 P–K5 N–R4** If 10 . . . P×P 11 B×P (threatening 12 B×N and 13 P–Q6) 11 . . . B–KN2 12 B–QB4 with an extremely active game for White. **11 Q–R4 B–Q2** Or 11 . . . Q–Q2? 12 N×P+! P×N 13 B–QN5, winning the queen. **12 P–K6! P×P 13 P×P B–B3** If 13 . . . N×B 14 P×B+ Q×P 15 N×P+ etc. winning, as in the previous note. Also hopeless is 13 . . . B×P 14 N–B7+ and 15 N×R. **14 N×P+! Q×N 15 B–QN5!** Q×P+ Or 15 . . . N–N1 16 Q×R N×B 17 B×B+ **16 B–K5** B×B **17 Q×B+ Q–Q2 18 Q×Q+ K×Q 19 B×R** White has a decisive material advantage.

The moral of this tale is 'beware of tactical possibilities beginning with the advance P–K5 by White'.

White Consolidates his Q-side Pawns

It is always important in a gambit opening for the side that sacrifices material to play actively. In the Benko Gambit the usual punishment for neglecting this rule is the setting up of white pawns on QN3 and QR4, possibly with a knight at QN5 for good measure. This formation normally puts paid to Black's counterplay and allows White to realise his material advantage.

143

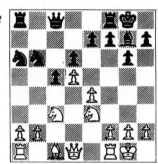

Doroshkevitch–Georgadze   Georgia–RSFSR, 1972

Here Black has played too tamely, in particular his queen is not at all active. **14 P–QR4 N–N5 15 R–R3 Q–R3 16 N–N5 Q–N2 17 P–QN3** In just four moves Black's Q-side counterattack has been neutralized. **17 ... P–B4 18 P×P P×P 19 Q–B5 Q–Q2 20 R–Q1 P–KB3 21 N–B4 N×N 22 P×N N–B7 23 R–R3 Q–B4 24 Q–K2** White is still a pawn up and he has the more active position. Black was unable to find sufficient counterplay and lost.

Sometimes when White plays the move P–QN3 he can fall victim to the counter ... P–QB5. The point is that if White exchanges pawns himself or allows Black to exchange on ... QN6 there will be an isolated Q-side pawn which needs protection for the remainder of the game and Black will have two open files on the Q-side along which he can operate. This idea of ... P–QB5 is, however, double-edged, since if White can meet ... P–QB5 with P–QN4 (now that he has already played P–QN3 White need not fear the en passent capture) he will have two connected passed pawns. This question of whether or not ... P–QB5 can be played with success after P–QN3 by White arises quite often in the Benko Gambit. The reader must be prepared to work out the pros and cons of ... P–QB5 for himself, depending on the circumstances.

White Pushes his Passed QRP

Finally, let us remind you that in the Benko Gambit Black gives up a pawn. If his counterplay proves ineffective he will find himself playing an ending in which White's passed QR-pawn is the decisive factor.

144

Khasin–Berezin   ½-final Moscow Ch 1962
White's advanced QR-pawn ties Black's light squared bishop to the role of
blockader. This pawn offers so much potential that White can afford to
give up the exchange in order to destroy the final vestiges of Black's
counterplay. **32 P×P! N–R6 33 P×P+ Q×P 34 Q–K4 N×R 35 N–N4!
B–N2 36 R×N R×P 37 R×R R×R 38 B–Q2 K–B1 39 N–R6 Q–B3 40
Q–R7 K–K1 41 N–N8 Q–B1 42 B–N5 R–N2 43 B–R5+ K–Q1 44 Q–N6
B–K4 45 B–R6 B–N2 46 Q×B Q×Q 47 B×Q P–B5 48 K–B2 P–K4 49 P×P
ep R×B 50 P–K7+ R×P 51 N×R K×N** The complications are over and
White still has his extra passed pawn. **52 K–K3 P–B6 53 B–N6 B–N4 54
B–Q3 B–R5 55 P–R6 K–Q2 56 P–R7 1–0** If 56 . . . B–B3 57 B–N5!

Index of Complete Games

This index includes all complete games and others of significant length which are of theoretical importance.

Bold indicates that a player had White.

FINAL POS. p. 2 L:F. AFTER 23... Qf4+

WH	BL.
Ke3	Kg8
Qb1	Qf4
Ra1	Bg7
Bf3	N's f6, c6
Ng3	P's a7, b7, f5,
P's a2 b2 c4	g6, h7
h2	

WH. to move

24. Ke2, Nd4+
25. Kd1, Qf3+
26. Kd2, Ne4+
27. Qe4, Bh6+
28. Ke1, fe4
29. Rc1, Bc1
30. b4, Nc2 ‡